The Long Haul

An Autobiography

Teachers College
Columbia University
New York and London

Published by Teachers College Press, 1234 Amsterdam Avenue,
New York, NY 10027

The photograph on the facing page is by Emil Willimetz.

Library of Congress Cataloging-in-Publication Data

Horton, Myles, 1905–
    The long haul : an autobiography / by Myles Horton with Judith
Kohl and Herbert Kohl.
        p. cm.
    Includes index.
    ISBN 0-8077-3700-3 (pbk. : alk. paper)
    1. Highlander Folk School (Monteagle, Tenn.)—History.
2. Horton, Myles, 1905–   . 3. School adminsitrators—Tennessee—
Biography. I. Kohl, Judith. II. Kohl, Herbert R. III. Title
LC5301.M65H69   1998
374′.9768′78—dc19   97-40870

ISBN 0-8077-3700-3

Printed on acid-free paper

Manufactured in the United States of America

11 10   9 8

Contents

Preface

The Long Haul was first published shortly after Myles Horton died in 1990, 58 years after he and several friends founded the Highlander Folk School in New Market, Tennessee.

What distinguishes Myles from many other people involved in social change over the past seventy years is his concern with education. Myles frequently asserted that he was not a leader or an organizer but an educator. He said that small victories are less important than the learning that can emerge from taking large risks. As an example, he said that it was wonderful to win a victory for a stop light, a new housing regulation, or an end to a toxic dump. But if in the course of that struggle you had learned nothing about the fundamental values you were struggling for or did not understand your own role in the process, you might end up becoming just another oppressor of people weaker than you are. If a victory in the building of working-class housing leads to the exclusion of people of color by a white community-based organization, or if a struggle to open a bank branch in a poor community ends in the gentrification of the community, the victories will turn into defeats in the long haul. Myles was concerned with people understanding things for themselves, based on their knowledge and experience, and Highlander in his mind was a learning place as well as a gathering place. Throughout his life Myles struggled to help people become morally and politically literate and never withheld himself from the dangers of their struggles, even at the risk of his life.

Myles Horton's long haul went uphill and it went downhill, as most difficult journeys do. Highlander's CIO labor organizing work in the 30s and 40s was unique and important. Its contribution to the

Civil Rights Movement in the 50's and 60's was monumental, particularly its role in developing citizenship schools, its support of leaders like Rosa Parks and Septima Clark, and its bringing together many of the young people—black and white—who fought to eliminate racial segregation in the South.

During the 70s and 80s, under the directorship of younger leaders but with Myles Horton vitally present, Highlander prepared dozens of ordinary citizens to research courthouse deeds and tax rolls for a vast study of who owns Appalachia's land, resources, and industry, an example of what has come to be known as participatory research. The Land Study eventually encouraged some state governments to demand higher taxes from corporations—often foreign owned—that were not paying their share of the costs of schools and roads and hospitals.

They helped workers with black and brown lung disease organize and demand health clinics and cleaner air in mines and textile mills. And they supported people who lived near toxic landfills and rivers polluted by strip mines and sawmills, showing them how to research the wastes and chemicals that polluters were dumping into the water and the ground. Then they helped them organize to stop the polluters.

When the young Myles Horton began his work there was already a growing movement to organize workers. Social Security was around the corner. Anti-trust legislation had been in effect for decades. As many of these worker and consumer protections are now disappearing into an epidemic of corporate mergers and flight to ever-cheaper labor, massive layoffs to increase corporate profits, huge public subsidies to lure private development, privately owned prisons with low-paid captive workers, constant pressure to weight environmental protection and health safeguards against profits, and callous denials that anyone has a responsibility to ensure a decent life for the poor, it is important to know that people have organized and won difficult battles in the past.

Myles Horton once said, "If you ever get to the place where injustice doesn't bother you, you're dead." For Myles there were plenty of people who were bothered, people whom he believed held invaluable knowledge about each unique problem they faced. It was his job to bring them together and provide a situation that would allow exchange and ultimately lead to some solutions.

—JUDITH KOHL AND HERBERT KOHL

How This Book Came About

In the spring of 1977 I devised a way to meet Myles Horton. I had never heard of either Myles or the Highlander Center until earlier that year. From 1962 to 1977 I had been teaching and writing about educational change and social and economic justice. The sixties and early seventies were exciting times for people who believed that it was possible to make fundamental changes in American society. Many of us felt that education could change people's lives, and that classrooms could be models of open, democratic living. A number of us, buoyed by the energy and hope provided by the civil rights movement, tried to take on the urban educational establishment. We hoped to obtain the means to create humane and decent schools, which would empower the children of the poor. What later became known as the "open classroom movement" was, for me, an extension of the civil rights struggles of the South into the classrooms of the North.

There were some temporary victories in those school wars, which made it possible to believe that real change was coming if only we persisted. The U.S. Office of Education even developed an Experimental Schools Program to support many people engaged in social reconstruction through the schools. In addition, resistance to the Vietnam War and the consequent infusion of young people with a social mission into teaching (many to avoid the draft) strengthened the notion that the schools could be effective agents for social change.

However, during the mid-seventies things began to return to "normal." With the end of the Vietnam War many "idealists" left teaching for more lucrative professions. The government turned

the Experimental Schools Program funds over to local school bureaucracies, which used them to destroy experimental schools and
replace them with authoritarian institutions. With the decrease in
federal funding for education that began in the Nixon years, many
school district budgets incurred deficits and used budget cutting as
a way to eliminate new programs, especially those that were successful and threatened the system as a whole.

Many decent educational programs were either eliminated or put
under such financial pressure that the struggle for survival destroyed
the energy and love needed for good teaching. It became increas-
ingly clear that the system didn't yield itself to reform as easily as
some of us had supposed it would. I had become convinced that
fundamental change was even more necessary than I had imagined,
but was also aware that the struggle for decency and justice could
easily consume a lifetime.

By 1977 I was determined to continue to work, in schools and
in society at large, for social and economic justice, but felt unsure
about how to go about it. I was also exhausted. I needed a teacher,
someone who knew more than I did about education, who had more
experience fighting for democracy and who could preserve humor
and compassion in the face of overwhelming opposition.

In the spring of that year, Joe Nathan, a friend and colleague,
sent me his review of Frank Adams' book, *Unearthing Seeds of Fire*,
about the Highlander Folk School. I read the book, which told the
story of Highlander's involvement in the industrial union and civil
rights movements. What struck me was the presence and voice of
Myles Horton throughout Highlander's history. He sounded like
the person I needed to know, and yet I was afraid to approach him
directly. Suppose he was a disappointment? What if he wasn't
interested in talking? I would have to observe him and decide whether
it made sense to try to learn from him.

I don't know why I felt so strongly about engineering a way to
observe Myles, but I went to great lengths to do it. That spring
there was to be a meeting in Chicago of the Alternative Schools
Network. The Brazilian educator Paulo Freire was invited there to
conduct a small community-based workshop, and money raised at
the conference would support Freire's workshop.

Jack Weise of the Network asked me to help him set up the
meeting, and I figured I might be able to use Freire's presence in
Chicago to lure Myles there. It was clear that if Myles was the

person I thought him to be, he would either know Freire and want to spend some time with him, or else he would know Freire's works and be anxious to meet him.

Since transportation for Freire and Myles would be expensive, I suggested the invitation of such prominent educators as John Holt, George Dennison and Eliot Wigginton. They had all written on humane schooling, and would make presentations at the conference. Their presence attracted about eight hundred people to the meeting, which more than covered all of the costs.

Then I called Myles and told him that Freire was coming to Chicago, and that the invitation committee hoped he could attend as well. He said he admired Freire's work and would be delighted to meet him. The only problem was that Myles said he didn't make formal presentations to large groups. After some talk we agreed that Myles would make an anecdotal presentation and take questions from the audience.

The night before the conference a number of us attended the first of Freire's workshops, conducted in a small church in one of Chicago's Hispanic communities. Most of the participants came from the neighborhood or from the Chicago alternative schools community. The sessions were planned by the community members and were supposed to deal with local needs and tensions.

Things moved very slowly. People were reluctant to speak, perhaps because there were so many strangers present. After a while, however, old neighborhood hostilities began to emerge. Some individuals began to express old animosities toward each other and resentment toward the guest "experts." The discussion had no focus, and I felt as if people had forgotten the purpose of being there, which was to solve pressing neighborhood problems. Just as I was afraid the whole situation would fall apart, an older man I hadn't noticed before, rather tall with gray hair, glasses and a thoroughly engaging if a bit wicked smile, got up and asked a question.

I can't remember the specific question, but do remember how it brought the group back to its purpose and got people focused on defining their problems and working toward a common solution.

I remember the Appalachian accent and also recall thinking that must be Myles. It was. I went to Myles' presentation at the conference the next day and listened to his stories and parables. They were very specific, very funny and always led to an educational insight. I also recall his talking about patience and how ingenuity can overcome blind power. And I hoped he would come to my presentation so that I could tell him something about myself and then, maybe, be invited to visit. I've never done anything like that before or since in my life.

Myles did show up and my presentation was made directly to him. I vaguely recollect that the theme was the search for stamina, and the pleasures provided by the people one works with. I talked about teaching, about my students, about values and morality and politics and education and change, just about everything that worried or delighted me in my educational work.

I didn't have a chance to talk to Myles until the moment I was about to take a taxi to the airport. I'd figured all of my scheming had been wasted and that I'd have to find another way to approach him. However, he came up to my cab and said, simply, "Why don't you come by Highlander sometime?"

My response was "Let's set a date," and we did.

To this day I don't know whether Myles' invitation was extended merely out of politeness. We've never talked about it. I do know that when I got home to California, I did something I've never done before. I urged my wife, Judy, to come with me to Highlander. Judy never went with me to educational meetings; however, this wasn't just a meeting. I expected our visit to Myles would have a major impact on our lives.

—HERBERT KOHL

The first visit Herb and I made to Highlander was in the fall of 1977. Although neither of us had a clear idea of what went on there, we had heard enough to think that we might learn something valuable about social change. Myles had retired from the directorship of Highlander in 1970, but he was then and still is host to a steady flow of friends and strangers whenever he isn't traveling around checking on the state of justice in the world. When we arrived after a nightlong flight from San Francisco, we were too excited to sleep, so Myles cooked up a big Southern breakfast and began a barrage of stories about his life and work. We took breaks to visit the school and library and to meet a number of Highlander staff members. Everyone was as welcoming as Myles, and as intense and committed to helping people get what needs to be done in the world done. "Long haul" people.

Early that evening, after another of Myles' unique meals—I remember a leg of lamb smeared with basil from his garden and a Horton-sized handful of garlic—we went down the hill to the center's main building for the evening session of a workshop in progress. For several days a group of men and women who suffer from black lung disease and brown lung disease had been meeting together with Highlander staff members and health care experts. These workers' health problems, which are caused by breathing unfiltered air in coal mines and textile mills, usually led to their being laid off, often long before retirement, and when this happened their health insurance benefits were terminated. The black-lung workers' advocacy groups had existed for some time, so their representatives were at Highlander to share their organizing experience with the brown-lung representatives, who were just beginning to search for ways to push the government and industry to restore their insurance benefits.

We found places in the rocking chairs that ringed the room and listened as Mike Clark (who had become Highlander's president and educational director in 1972) quietly brought up ideas and raised questions. People talked about their perceptions of the problems, the ways they might be able to solve some of them and about the progress some groups were already making.

After years of involvement in confrontational education politics in New York and California, we found this process of quiet but earnest inquiry shocking. People listened to each other. You could almost touch the caring and intelligence in the room. Mike is a tall, fast-talking man with an edge of suppressed rage in his voice. At the same time he managed to be gentle and funny, like Myles clearly comfortable with the workshop participants.

Since this was an evening session, there was more than talk. Candie and Guy Carawan and Phyllis Boyans were there to bring people together in song, to get to a place beyond the factual recounting of events and organizing for the future.

Then we all watched a film about the organization of a coal strike, *Harlan County, U.S.A.*, which Highlander had a hand in making. Later everyone got up from their rocking chairs as Mike started a square dance, a slow, subdued one for these victims of a disease that would never have hit them if the operators of the mines and textile mills where they worked had installed adequate safety equipment.

Myles began telling his story to us during that first trip to Highlander, but it wasn't until somewhat later that Herb began to record it. Since then Myles has visited us in California several times. For about two weeks in 1985, he stayed with us and our three children in London. It was at this time that I became involved in the book project. All six of us traveled to Wales to meet people active in the National Union of Miners who had visited Highlander to meet with American miners. They were part of an international network of workers Myles and Highlander have helped develop. I made two more trips to Highlander to record more material; Herb did the same on four other occasions. During the time we spent with Myles, most of our conversations weren't recorded at all. The majority weren't even directly relevant to the book that was slowly taking form. We would find ourselves having to end far-ranging conversations at the kitchen table and to force ourselves to pull out the tape recorder and get to work. Altogether we recorded many hours of Myles' ideas, stories and history.

It was a long journey from our intention to write a book about Myles Horton's educational and philosophical ideas to the realization that the whole story was there, or almost there, in Myles' own words. So, *The Long Haul* became Myles' book. Whenever the recording sessions got under way, there were few interruptions by Herb or me, just a question or two to set the direction. Sometimes we needed to go back and forth to get more material, because we hadn't always known, especially at the beginning, the right questions to ask and what form the book would ultimately take. At Myles' suggestion we also included some of his previously written and spoken words. (These are identified in the text.) As we finally pieced the sections together, Myles patiently and carefully went over them, and when we thought the book was finished he reviewed it one last time.

For more detailed history of the Highlander Folk School, consult John M. Glen's *Highlander: No Ordinary School, 1932–1962* (Lexington, Ky.: The University Press of Kentucky, 1988), and Frank Adams' *Unearthing Seeds of Fire: The Idea of Highlander* (Winston-Salem, N.C.: John F. Blair, 1975), with Myles Horton.

We want to thank a number of people who have been connected with Highlander over the years for their help and encouragement: Candie Carawan; Guy Carawan; Courtney Cazden; John Gaventa; Aimee Isgrig Horton, whose University of Chicago Ph.D. thesis on Highlander written during the 1960s has been an invaluable resource; Charis Horton; Helen Lewis; Tom Ludwig; Juliet Merrifield; Lucy Phenix, especially for her 1985 film on Highlander, *You Got to Move*; Anne Lockwood Romasco; Sue Thrasher; and the people at the Highlander Library.

We are also grateful to Judy Austermiller; Cynthia Stokes Brown; Joseph Featherstone; Colin Greer; John Hurst; Nancy Mikelsons; Joe Nathan; and, for her incomparable transcribing skills, Anne Newkirk Niven.

Mike Clark was generous with his time and insight, and made some important suggestions that we tried our best to implement.

The State Historical Society of Wisconsin was most helpful with background material from the Highlander Collection. The Boehm Foundation and the New World Foundation provided welcome financial support.

We also want to thank our agent Wendy Weil for her support and enthusiasm, and our editor Sally Arteseros for the energy and commitment she brought to this book.

Finally, our children Antonia, Erica and Joshua, whose lives have been enriched by visits from Myles, deserve thanks for all the questions they raised and for their many valuable insights. We thank them too for being the kind of people who understand the importance of what Myles Horton and Highlander have to say and do about how people can live in the world.

—JUDITH KOHL

Introduction

In the Appalachian coalfields a young woman organizes the women in her community to play a vital part in the upcoming coal strike.

In Alabama a group of black farmers is raising oats to send to Nicaragua.

In a small rural community in southwest Virginia, women work to develop a community-owned factory to replace a runaway plant that has been relocated to a foreign country.

In Mississippi a young man organizes an oral history project to learn about the civil rights movement that he and his generation missed.

In Louisiana a man organizes a group to research the chemical hazards affecting the community.

Off the coast of South Carolina a group of traditional singers work to preserve their music and teach the children about their heritage.

All these people have in some way been influenced by Myles Horton and the Highlander education program, which he began in the mountains of Tennessee in 1932.

Highlander Folk School, later renamed Highlander Research and Education Center, has educated three generations of activists who worked in the labor and civil rights movements in the South and Appalachia. It has also been a major catalyst for social change in the United States for almost sixty years.

Seeking to develop a form of education to change society rather than maintain the status quo, Myles Horton created a pedagogy which leads people to challenge the system, to take risks. Myles calls it a "two-eye" theory of teaching. He keeps one eye on where people are, and one eye on where they can be—forever pushing, making them uncomfortable, stretching their minds, helping them grow in their understanding and critical consciousness.

Myles, now eighty-four years old, continues to educate. This book is the story of how he learned from his experiences and developed his particular theory of education.

Myles Horton grew up in the rural South in the first quarter of the century. His philosophy, educational theory and values have deep roots in his Southern rural experiences. His family was from the hills of Tennessee. They were members of the Cumberland Presbyterian Church, a strongly egalitarian, frontier, anti-elitist denomination. From his family he inherited a down-to-earth theology, an old-time "primitive Christianity," which was simple, straight, hard-nosed, with clear ideas of right and wrong. His grandfather gave him a strong biblical sense of the differences between rich and poor, and his mother instilled the importance of love and service. He was smart and proud, encouraged to read, learn and question. He had no sense of inferiority, and he approached life with a country arrogance, questioning and confronting ideas and issues in church, school and work. He was influenced by his experiences on the farm, in factories and sawmills, working with the Student YMCA in college, and teaching Bible in rural schools. Through these experiences he became committed to fighting injustices and working to make the South more democratic. Later, at Union Theological Seminary, at the University of Chicago and at Danish folk schools, he developed his educational ideas and plans for an adult education center.

One of the most important elements of Highlander pedagogy is the recognition that the best teachers of poor and working people are the people themselves. Rather than bringing in "experts" as resource people, Highlander brings people together, developing a circle of learners who share the same problems. Together people share their experiences, analyze their problems and learn how to work toward basic changes in society. The goal is not reform or adjustment to an unjust society but the transformation of society.

It is an education for action. It is dangerous education; and although much emphasis is on forming strategies to confront the system without being destroyed, people are encouraged to push the boundaries, to be creative in solving problems. Often this means pushing to the place where they get into trouble. Myles insists that until people take some risks and gain some independence from the system, they are not free to learn or to act. As people try to be part of the decision-making process, they discover that *learning* about democracy involves *working* to replace, transform and rebuild society to allow for equal participation.

Although Myles developed this method of education from his own life and work with poor and working people in the rural South, it is not unique to Highlander and to Myles. Paulo Freire in Brazil and Julius Nyerere in Tanzania learned these lessons independently. Others working in similar situations in Chile, Colombia, India, Nicaragua, Kenya and Europe have developed a similar pedagogy by observing how people learn and tying this to the need for basic changes in society.

Today there is a flowering of this philosophy. Oppressed and poor people all over the world who haven't been empowered before are being brought into the development process. People are asking hard questions of governments and the economic system.

In recent years Myles has worked to build networks with people in popular education movements all over the world. Other Highlander staff members have been active in international adult education and participatory research groups working to link these movements. People from the rural South, making real changes toward a more democratic society, are sharing their experiences with others struggling to change their communities. As people all over the earth use education for social transformation, they are generating an international social movement for political participation and change. Myles Horton and Highlander are among the vital headwaters of this mighty human stream.

—HELEN M. LEWIS

You can hitch your wagon to the stars, but you can't haul corn or hay in it if its wheels aren't on the ground.

—MORDECAI PINKNEY HORTON
1858–1934

ONE

Beginnings

I was born in Savannah, Tennessee, on July 9, 1905. Before I was born my mother and father had both been schoolteachers, in the days before you had to go to college to be a schoolteacher. Later on they did odd jobs, worked in canning factories, sold insurance. My father was a county clerk at one time, then a sharecropper. We didn't think of ourselves as working-class, or poor, we just thought of ourselves as being conventional people who didn't have any money.

My grandfather was an illiterate mountain man who was born

before the Civil War. He said that the only reason he didn't learn to read and write was that at the time he was supposed to go to school, there weren't any schools, and it never occurred to him, after he was grown, to go to school. The idea of lifelong learning just wasn't there. He wasn't embarrassed about the fact that he couldn't read or write. He had a keen mind and from him I learned to respect people who weren't literate, in the technical sense. He could do complicated fractions in his head. He bought and sold cattle, and when he looked at a cow he could weigh her in his mind. He'd multiply that weight by the category, young or old, she fitted into, and know, within a couple of dollars, what he could get for her in the market that day, according to market prices. And he'd offer under that. Before he left in the morning, he'd say to me, "Son, read today's cattle prices report," and I'd read something from each category. If I repeated anything, he'd say, "You've already read it."

You have to respect a mind like that. Because of him I've always understood there is a difference between being able to read and being intelligent.

My grandfather was always saying, "Well, that's for rich people." "Rich people do that." "Rich people do this." And "That's not for poor people." He thought rich people were evil and were going to hell. He had a very clear idea of rich and poor: the rich were people who lived off of somebody else. The people he knew who worked and lived on their own were mostly poor.

He didn't want to be one of the rich. It is difficult for some people to understand that there are workers, good people, who don't want to imitate the rich, don't even want to be rich. They want to live decently on the basis of their work and don't respect the rich for being rich.

With that kind of background, I grew up not even questioning that poor people were good and rich people bad. I didn't know why until I started making my own living, when I was fifteen and still going to school. I worked as a clerk in a store and started to see how unequal the wage system was. My first feeling about it was that it was very unjust for somebody to have to work so hard and get so little, and for somebody else to have so much.

From my mother and father I learned the idea of service and the value of education. They taught me by their actions that you are supposed to serve your fellow men, you're supposed to do some-

Savannah, Tennessee. Aunt Martha, seated; Myles Horton with his parents, Elsie Falls Horton and Perry Horton. *MH, personal collection.*

thing worthwhile with your life, and education is meant to help you do something for others. I learned that not so much by words but by demonstration. One time when we were pretty hard up, Dad got a job in a tomato factory in the little town of Humboldt in West Tennessee. It was also a cotton mill town, and my mother would go over a couple times a week to a mill where the people were really in terrible shape. Most of them were not literate and there was a lot of sickness. She'd go over there and take some food, and afterward she'd hold a kind of Bible class. We wouldn't have very much for supper that night. Like any kid I might have resented it, but I really don't remember feeling that way. I know it meant so much to her and I wouldn't have wanted to hurt her feelings by complaining. She was that kind of a woman, she shared out of her poverty.

There are many examples of mother's way of helping people.

Shortly after the Highlander Folk School was started in 1932 in Monteagle, Tennessee, my mother and father were still partially employed, partially unemployed. Dad was working for the Works Progress Administration (WPA), so they decided to come up and live in the county where Highlander was located. My mother could help with the cooking, and Dad with the garden. As soon as she got there, Mom became terribly concerned about the high birthrate around Monteagle—the families just kept having more kids and the kids were hungry half the time. She started telling people about birth control, and it was very unpopular. They had thought Mom was a good Christian and here she was advocating birth control.

There was a woman there who had seven kids all about the same age, and Mom decided she'd talk to her, so she invited her over to her house one day and started a little propaganda, and this woman said, "Oh, I don't agree with that. My father was a minister and Baptist preacher and we're against that kind of thing." She didn't want to hear any more about it, so Mom just changed the subject. She wasn't put out, it just hadn't worked.

Four kids and four years later this same woman came back. My mother was on the porch again, and this woman came in and sat down by her and said, "Mom, what was you talking about the other day?" And Mom just finished the sentence and went on as if nothing had happened.

She was the best-loved person around there. I've always antagonized people with some things I do. I make enemies as well as friends, and I take strong positions, but people always liked Mom, even if it took them several years to want her to finish a sentence. They'd always come back.

Dad was an interesting person, but he wasn't the socially active person my mother was. He was always on the right side though: he joined the union and worked in a cooperative. One time after I was in college, the family was getting ready to move for some reason. Before they decided where to go, he sat down and wrote letters to five counties, asking what kind of high schools they had for my sister, Elsie Pearl and brothers, Dan and Delmas. Then he picked the county that sounded the best and moved there without a job, just because of the schools. He had a real interest in our getting an education.

Dad was a member of the Workers' Alliance, the union of WPA workers. He used to tell stories on the job. The workers would sit around listening to him at lunchtime and nobody would want to go back to work. Sometimes a boss would complain about Dad telling stories all the time and order him to get to work. Sometimes he'd run out of stories and make up some more, but he told the old ones over and over again. Strangely enough, people like to hear familiar stories. I guess that's where I picked up storytelling.

Dad was also a fox hunter. Fox hunting in the mountains consists of having the dogs chase and bark after the fox, but they must never catch him, because if they kill the fox they can't come back next week. The fox hunters did what they called "listening to the music." They knew each dog's sound: "That's old Sue, that's Tuck." It's a game the foxes are in on. They know that they can never get caught because they can go into their dens and the dogs will go home.

I went on one of the fox hunts one time in the moonlight. Down under the ridge where I was, I saw a fox jump up on a rail fence and go for about two city blocks and then jump off the fence and head back the way he had come. The hounds were coming after him on his scent. I saw them walk over to the rail fence and turn back. Then they started yelping. They hunted around for an hour, trying to pick up his trail. They didn't think about going back where they'd been, because they'd just been there. I was never too concerned about the foxes, I was concerned about the dogs getting tired. When the foxes got tired, they'd go into their holes.

I still have a photograph of Dad with his hounds. Once when they were puppies—Nip and Tuck were their names—I heard Dad cussing and screaming. I ran over and asked him what was happening, and he said, "It's going to swallow them." "It" was a little snake about twice as long as the puppies and as thick as your thumb. Dad was just beating on him. Swallow his puppies! They were important to him.

Our family was in the Cumberland Presbyterian Church. When the Presbyterians first came into the mountains, they had a very stiff, formal church, but they weren't making much headway be-

Perry and Elsie Horton with foxhounds, 1937. *MH, personal collection. Marion Post.*

cause they didn't have enough preachers who knew Latin and Greek. They couldn't compete with the Baptists and Methodists after the great revivals that started in New England came down here, so they started a people's Presbyterian church. Still, they kept all the Calvinist theology, including a belief in predestination: things God preordained to happen would happen.

I ran across some of the old theology books in my grandparents' attic and started reading them when I was in grammar school. One day I went to my mother and said, "I don't know, this predestination doesn't make any sense to me, I don't believe any of this. I guess I shouldn't be in this church."

Mom laughed and said, "Don't bother about that, that's not important, that's just preachers' talk. The only thing that's important is you've got to love your neighbor." She didn't say, "Love God," she said, "Love your neighbor, that's all it's all about." She had a very simple belief: God is love, and therefore you love your neighbors. Love was a religion to her, that's what she practiced. It was a good nondoctrinaire background, and it gave me a sense of what was right and what was wrong.

I've taken this belief of my mother's and put it on another level, but it's the same idea. It's the principle of trying to serve people and building a loving world. If you believe that people are of worth, you can't treat anybody inhumanely, and that means you not only have to love and respect people, but you have to think in terms of building a society that people can profit most from, and that kind of society has to work on the principle of equality. Otherwise, somebody's going to be left out.

People always ask, "Can we wait till we have a society that's perfect to have equality?" Well, of course, we'll never achieve it unless we start where we are, so you begin incorporating principles of equality into everything you do. That's complicated, because it's hard to avoid domination or inequality, or paternalism: but the principle itself isn't complicated, it's the application that's complicated.

When you work toward equality, you have to devise some kind of structure in which there can be justice, but in the meantime you have to do the best you can in an unjust society. Sometimes that means that the laws you go by are moral laws instead of book laws. It isn't too complicated to get the principles of equality and justice and love, but to make these things function, you have to trust that people have the capacity to live that way and to achieve that kind of society. This is hard to do, because under present day conditions many people are untrustworthy. They are untrustworthy in a temporary sense. In the potential sense they are trustworthy, so you have to posit trust in spite of the fact that the people you're dealing with don't, on the surface, merit that trust, and they will never merit it until you have it in all the people. It's the kind of thing you just have to posit: you have to have trust in people, and you have to work through it to the place where people respond to that trust. Then you have to believe that people have the capacity within themselves to develop the ability to govern themselves.

By the time I was fifteen I had to leave home to go to school because there wasn't a high school in the county where we lived. After a while my father and mother decided if they were going to starve they might as well starve where there was a school, so they moved to where I was in the Forkadeer River Valley. I could live at home again, but I kept on working because I had a part-time job and Dad didn't.

I learned a lot growing up. My people were farmers, sharecroppers, factory workers, clerks—anything to make a living. When I heard people insulted by the factory owners, it hurt me personally. I didn't feel a bit inferior to the guy who owned the factory. I felt just as smart, in fact I knew I was smarter than he was. Who was *he* to talk about people like me and my family? I guess I got as much help from the opposition in firming up my beliefs as I did from more positive sources.

Another job I had when I was fifteen was working in a sawmill. It was a dangerous and low-paying job where you could get your arms or your legs cut off, and people did. After a while I asked around about how you got a better job. This was a little sawmill downriver in West Tennessee. We worked in the swamps, cutting cypress logs. Somebody told me that if you challenged a man with a better job to a wrestling match and you threw him, then he'd lose his job and you'd get it.

I had a cousin who was bigger than I was, and I made him wrestle with me all the time. I'd chase him down because I'd want to practice. Then one Saturday I challenged a guy at the mill. He was about thirty-five years old, bigger than me, and I threw him. I still didn't know if it was true he'd lose his job. I went back to

Myles Horton (center) with his brothers: Delmas (left) and Dan Horton, 1914. *MH, personal collection.*

work on Monday and the boss told me to take this guy's job. That's how we dealt with problems in my first job. Not collectively, just individually.

My next work experience was making crates to ship tomatoes in. We built those crates right in front of the packers. We'd get half a penny a crate, so you can imagine how many we'd have to make to earn any money. The work went very fast, and not many people could make them fast enough for the workers who nailed them shut. Other workers in the factory were getting paid a lot more money than we were, so we decided to ask for a raise. I analyzed the situation: if there aren't any crates, no one can pack the tomatoes, and tomorrow when the farmers bring in another load, the tomatoes will pile up and the owners will lose money. So I got the other kids to stop making crates and we organized a union. I didn't know it was a union. I don't think any of us knew about unions. We just got together and said that we wanted more money, because everybody else was getting a lot but us. When they said no, we just quit.

The owners couldn't believe it. They said, "Well, we'll just get someone else," and we replied, "Go ahead, there isn't anybody else who can make these crates in this town. We're the only ones in this town fast enough to make them, and there aren't any other towns around here."

They said, "No, you can't quit," so we took about two hours off. The tomatoes kept stacking up until we got a raise. That must have been in 1922, because I was still in high school.

A couple of years later, I worked in a box factory. They didn't have a union either, but they had work control, which consisted of everybody agreeing to set a pace and not get any faster. But I didn't know that when I started work. Now, in this factory, my job was to take a piece of veneer that had a little groove in it and bend it so the people on the machine could make strawberry baskets out of it. It hurt my fingers and I had to work hard to keep up, but then I found that if you took about ten pieces of veneer and leaned the heel of your hand on them and put your body down easy you could do the job better than if you made the grooves one at a time.

I was working ten times faster than the way they taught me to do it and doing a better job, so I thought I was helping the other workers. The line was set for me to do one at a time, so the rest of the time I'd fiddle around. When the workers saw my pace, one of them came over and said, "Look, Myles, you're doing this work so fast they'll make you do two jobs." They were teaching me some things the older workers already knew. The more work you did, the more work you'd get, but the pay would be the same.

The supervisor in that plant had previously been a worker, and the reason he was the supervisor was that all the people liked him. He devised a system of not working too hard while still making money for the company. He saw what I was doing, and he came over and said, "Myles, your system is great, but you're going to mess things up for everybody else. You come over to my booth and read when you get your quota done."

He knew I liked books, because I was known as the town reader. In his office he had all of the Knickerbocker series and James Fenimore Cooper's *Leatherstocking Tales*, Washington Irving's stories—a whole shelf of books—so I sat in his booth and read after I'd done two or three hundred boxes and stacked them up. He was the only supervisor, so nobody else knew what went on. As long as I stayed off the production line when the boss came, it was fine. Nobody wanted the boss to see this young fella standing there doing nothing. Everyone was protecting everybody else.

Besides reading, I played defensive tackle on the high school football team. I learned how to knife through the other school's line and attack the fullback before he got started. What happened was that I was lighter—although I was faster—than the average high school player, so I couldn't just use my weight against the other guy. I had to figure out other angles. What I did was to analyze, by trial and error, the way the opposition tackle functioned. I found his method of operating and I'd play into it as if I didn't know it and he had all the advantages because he was doing it his way, using his weight against me. I'd do that two or three times and every time he'd knock me down. When I got him conditioned, I would feign doing what I had always done, and he'd lunge ahead. It was then just a simple matter of grabbing him by the shoulders and throwing him to the ground and walking through the hole. In fact, I became famous for making tackles behind the line.

Once, we were about to play a very tough team, much bigger than ourselves. I was walking down from the locker room to the football field, right by a place where I had planted a lot of flowers. Other people were planting flowers around the campus, and I thought, "Hell, if they're planting them everywhere else, we might as well have them around the football field, too." One of the guys from the other team was walking along being friendly and talking to me, but when we got near the field, he asked, "What're these sissy flowers doing here by a football field?" I didn't say anything, but I was just boiling inside. It turned out he was their star fullback. I played my usual game of psyching the opposition out and letting them clobber me two or three times, and I watched him as he started out running high. When he got close to the line, he'd do what a football player is supposed to—get low—but he didn't do it until he'd gotten almost to the line. I figured if I could move through fast enough and get him before he tucked in, I could lay him out with a flying tackle. I did it—he took the ball from the quarterback and stood straight up and he wasn't ready for my tackle and was knocked out cold. The game was called.

I helped carry him up to the locker room—we didn't have any

11

stretchers, we just picked people up by their arms and legs and carried them off. I had a terrible feeling about this guy and his contempt for flowers and how he insinuated that anybody who cared about them was a sissy. He was half unconscious, but I couldn't resist the temptation to dump him into the flower bed. As he fell, I said, "Smell 'em!"

TWO

College

In 1924 I got encouragement from our church to attend Cumberland University in Lebanon, Tennessee. I probably profited by going to a small college where I didn't have many good teachers. The college had a fairly good library, so I learned to educate myself. If I'd had to spend time with good teachers, I probably wouldn't have come out as well educated as I did.

While at college, I did have two fine teachers. One of them was my English professor, who didn't know anything about teaching but loved literature. That was all I needed, somebody who would cheer me on, somebody who was glad I liked books and would be there to talk to me when I wanted to discuss what I was reading.

The other teacher was a young sociologist just out of the University of Chicago. While I was in his class, I wrote a paper on a tobacco workers' cooperative that was organized in the twenties by a New Yorker who had come down to live in Kentucky. He didn't know anything about agriculture, but he knew about cooperatives and militant organizing strategies. He got the farmers together and they built an effective farmers' cooperative. It was interesting to me because he was an outsider who had come into an area and was able, through his knowledge and skills, to put together a bunch of individualistic farmers. In my paper I tried to figure out how he organized them. I was interested in the cooperative. I also wanted to make the teacher understand that I could use his help and that I really wanted to learn. When I got the paper back, I read one of his margin comments next to a source I had quoted: "It isn't who said it that's important, but is it true?" He was saying, "Don't just give me authorities for this, you tell me why it's true." Now that to me is a good teacher.

For the rest I had plenty of time to read. Four years of reading! I'm serious when I say that I probably got a better education by not having good teachers than if I had had teachers who I thought knew things. I would have had to listen to them and learn their opinions, instead of developing my own.

I played football in college, but I quit because it was interfering with my reading. In fact, the administration threatened to prevent me from graduating if I left the team, but I went on reading anyway. Learning was more important than graduating.

In college I was active in the Student YMCA, which was involved in working for racial equality as well as other aspects of social and economic justice. At that time there were interracial commissions in the South, and some of the students in the Student YMCA (a more liberal branch of the YMCA) and the YWCA were making efforts to deal with prejudice by having blacks and whites of good will sit down together and talk. In order not to antagonize people and narrow their opportunities to bring in all kinds, the students accepted the customs of the South. The blacks and whites wouldn't drink coffee together or eat together. They followed all the Jim Crow patterns while they talked about them. Before I got out of

Myles Horton at Cumberland University, 1927. *MH, personal collection.*

college I had rejected this approach as being counterproductive. I was working on the idea that you learn what you do, and not what you talk about.

Even before Highlander Folk School started, I was committed to breaking the pattern of segregation and to practicing social equality. I wanted action to be the main thrust, instead of just talking about future action that you don't practice. Practice what you preach, in other words. That was clear to me in the 1920s, and I started agitating.

The year I graduated from college I had a job as a state Student YMCA secretary, and I began to get into all kinds of trouble because I was putting my convictions into practice. In order to act on my beliefs I had to accept the idea of civil disobedience. I knew that I might have to violate those laws that were unjust, and I made up my mind never to do something wrong just because it was legal. My conscience would help me decide what was right and wrong, not the law. I made that decision in college. Thus, I was clear on civil disobedience and I was clear on action taking precedence over talk. This meant that I couldn't work with interracial leadership people—blacks or whites—because they were all committed to gradualism.

I also knew that if people have a position on something and you try to argue them into changing it, you're going to strengthen that position. If you want to change people's ideas, you shouldn't try to convince them intellectually. What you need to do is get them into a situation where they'll have to act on ideas, not argue about them.

Before I got my job with the Student YMCA there were three high schools that had branch clubs. Within six months I managed to organize another twelve clubs, nine in white high schools and three in black high schools. In those days blacks and whites weren't allowed to go to school together, so none of the clubs were integrated. They could meet jointly, but they couldn't eat or socialize with each other in any way.

I was trying to break the pattern of segregation and decided to organize a statewide convention where everyone could meet and eat together. I knew it was illegal, and I knew that if I let the students and the schools know beforehand, they'd be against the convention. I decided to convene it anyway, but not on a school-by-school basis. I just gave one of the statewide student officers a list of people to invite, and he sent out individual invitations.

The conference was to begin with a banquet at a whites-only hotel in downtown Knoxville. I made reservations for the banquet but didn't tell anyone that we were an integrated group. I didn't say we weren't one, either—I just didn't say. I leveled with no one, but I did tell the truth, which was that we were going to have a banquet.

The first time people realized what was happening was when we gathered at the hotel for the banquet. I arranged for us all to come in the street door that led directly into the banquet room. That way, we avoided going through the lobby and creating a stir before we even sat down to eat.

The situation became a reality when we sat down at the tables. Now, if you confront people with a reality that is different from the one they are used to and they don't know how not to do what they're supposed to in a given situation, they won't know how to act. When we entered the dining room the black kids started looking around and the white kids started looking around. They were all the same age, they were all Y members. They did what they were used to doing in a dining room—they sat down to eat. They did the familiar in an unfamiliar situation. I'm not sure they even gave it much thought at that moment.

Then the waiters came in. They were all black. And they said, "We can't serve you because we can't serve black and white people together."

"These are just a bunch of high school kids, what do you mean you can't serve them, they're fine. Just bring out the food."

The waiters insisted again that they couldn't serve us, so I told them I didn't understand. "We're paying you to serve us. We hired you to wait on us. If we get up and leave, you'll go home without any pay, and if we don't get any food, we'll all get up and leave." Now there were about 120 of us, and I asked the waiters what they were going to do with all that food for 120 that was already cooked. They answered that they couldn't make the decision to feed us. I told them to inform whomever could make that decision what the problem was.

They fed us.

That was in 1928, long before any civil rights movement activity in Knoxville. At the hotel everybody was confronted. I took a gamble: we could have been arrested; we could have been thrown out; the kids could have walked out; the waiters could have walked out. I took the gamble of doing something about a moral problem instead of simply talking about it. I just reversed the process that was going on in the universities and churches, and over 120 people learned that they could change things if they wanted to.

THREE

Learning

I remember a time at Cumberland University when I was trying to work out a problem about a program for the Y, and couldn't think of what to do. There were a couple of students from New Jersey in the house where I lived. They had been looking for an inexpensive college and found out about Cumberland because the Presbyterian church had a base in New Jersey. They were new students and didn't know anything about what was going on in the college. Their whole background, which was Jewish, was altogether different from ours. It never occurred to me to talk to them about our regional problems. One night we were just sitting around. I was pretty depressed and one of them said, "What are you bothered about? You've been kind of sitting there trying to figure out something." I said, "Oh, I'm just thinking about something."

"Just out of curiosity, what is it?"

When I finally told them, they were fascinated. We started talking and they gave me a lot of good suggestions, not directly, but I could take their ideas and turn them around and put them in the context of my problems. I'd transpose and translate what they were saying, and in a little while I'd come out with a good program. If it wasn't for them, I'd have been trapped by my own ideas, which weren't helping to solve the problem. I didn't think anything about it at the time, but later on I said, "My God, what's happened? Here I've been trying to be a loner, trying to do this all by myself and never thinking about asking anybody else."

That was the beginning of my learning how to talk to others and getting help from them. I learned to listen and turn people's ideas around in my mind. They were experts on their own lives and their own experiences. And those experiences could have something to teach me even if I didn't see it at the moment.

During two summers while I was at Cumberland, I had a job with the Presbyterian church in their Sunday school and daily vacation Bible school program as the student field representative in four Cumberland Mountain Plateau counties. The first year, I did what I was told to do, which was to visit some of the Sunday schools and try to revive them, and to set up and run daily vacation Bible schools for the children.

At the same time, I started to spend time with Rev. Abram Nightingale, the minister of a Congregational church in Crossville. He was always friendly to outsiders because he was an outsider himself. He took in wandering students and hoboes and always shared whatever he had. He had come from New Jersey after going to a very conservative theological seminary, Moody Bible Institute, but he wasn't a conservative; he was a freethinking, independent sort of man who wasn't charismatic at all. The church to him was more or less a means of making a living while he helped people. He didn't think it was that central to the teachings of Jesus, so he worked in the hospital emptying bedpans and doing other things that nobody else would do, and spent time helping farmers with their everyday problems. I was attracted by what I thought was a kind of sainthood he had in comparison to other preachers I'd known.

It was through him that I met a lot of people I would not have ordinarily met: the county agent, Bob Lyons, who was interested in setting up cooperatives, and a young fellow who had a job with the county and was teaching people to build privies and to test their water.

My interests extended beyond the Bible school job. I realized the church was just making jobs for college students and didn't expect them to do very much. I asked the head of the program how many daily vacation Bible schools he expected me to run in the summer and he gave me a number, so I assumed that once I had them going smoothly, the rest of the time was my own. The second year, I was assigned two women student assistants who loved working with the kids and were very good at it. I got some recruits to help them, so the program had about a half dozen people who loved to teach young children while I did other things.

Sometimes I'd visit an Episcopal minister who lived in Harriman, about thirty to forty miles away. Once a month he'd go up to a little place called Rugby, formerly a Christian Socialist colony, and hold church services. When I went down to spend the weekend with him one time, he was too sick to go. He asked me if I'd go in his place and hold the service. I told him, "I can't do that, I'm not a minister, I've never ever been in an Episcopalian church. I don't know anything about it." He said, "The service is all written down; we just read it. I wish you'd go up because those people will be terribly disappointed. I don't have any way to get word there. They come down to pick me up, and I can't get word to them not to come down, but they could take you up instead." I said, "Yes, but they want the Lord talking to them and they know who I am. They know I'm not the right person." He finally convinced me it would be an interesting thing to do, and I put on his robe and went up to Rugby and read the service, just like that minister. And those people all knew me well enough to realize I didn't believe a word of it. It didn't bother them in the least—they liked me personally—and they just accepted the fact that I was an actor.

In my second year there I decided I wanted to experiment a bit. I was helping with the daily vacation Bible school in a small church out in the country near Ozone. Ozone is a little community in the

Cumberland Mountains. It has a post office, a waterfall and about three or four houses. The church was on a creek approximately four or five miles away. Once we had the people sending their kids to the Bible school, I decided I was going to try an experiment that would take into consideration some of the things I'd learned from working with Bob Lyons and Rev. Nightingale, and from getting to know some miners, miners' union members, and some textile workers who had gone off to work outside the mountains and come back because they had been fired or developed bad lungs. Agriculture was pretty much like it is today in the sense that the farmers were barely hanging on. That was about 1927: the Depression hit the rural South a long time before it was felt in New York.

I wanted to deal with some of those problems that I was becoming aware of, so what I did was to pass the word that I'd like all the parents and other adults to come to a meeting. I didn't tell them what it was going to be about. They just thought it had something to do with the daily vacation Bible school or with the church. When we got them there, we spent about five minutes talking about the daily vacation Bible school—it's the kind of approach the community-based priests use now, in Central and South America. They get the people talking about the Bible and then get them into discussions about organizing and revolution. I was doing the same thing by starting out with the religious part of the meeting, then telling them, "I want you people to know everything's going fine, the kids are in good shape, we've been having some good recreation programs"—I'd been teaching them to swim—and then I said that I'd been working around this part of the country for the past two years and wondered if we could spend a little time talking about some of the things I'd been seeing, such as sanitation projects, co-ops, and so on. I had to do a lot of probing to get them started talking, because though they may have talked about these things individually or been to co-op or union meetings, they'd probably never been to a community-wide meeting where such topics were discussed. It was a little awkward for all of us, but the people finally started talking about their problems and what they were up against.

They looked to me for help, thinking I had started the discussion because I had money or seeds to give them, or some service to provide. As it went along I got skittish and really worried. I could see they were bringing these things out because they hoped I had answers to their problems, but although I had concern for their problems I had no answers. Finally, I told them that I hadn't called this meeting because I had answers. I didn't know the answers and I didn't have any technical competence. Instead, I told a story of how when I was growing up we used to sit around in our house or other peoples' houses and people would talk about their problems just like this. Somebody would say, "Try this . . ." or "I heard about this . . ." and a lot of ideas and knowledge would come out when people talked to each other.

Before the meeting was over I had made a very valuable discovery. You don't have to know the answers. The answers come from the people, and when they don't have any answers, then you have another role, and you find resources: I knew Bob Lyons, and if the people were interested in getting together in a co-op, I could get Bob to come out there, and if they had a sanitation problem, they could work with another man who could help them build privies. I had a list of items in my mind that I hadn't thought of when I went in there, but I just knew them from working with these people. So I became a resource person and started setting up follow-up meetings.

The word spread about that meeting and we had one every night. So many people came that when I made a report of the total number in attendance at this little country church, I had the names of about seventy-five or eighty individuals. Dr. Warren Wilson, a friend and Presbyterian church official who had taught at Union Theological Seminary, wrote me a letter and said, "Myles, you have a very good reputation and we're all proud of you, but somebody brought your last report to me and said you were exaggerating and that nobody ever got that many people at a meeting, in fact he said there weren't that many people living around there. I think you ought to change the report, say '20' or something. That's hard enough to swallow." I told him it was true that there weren't so many people in the immediate vicinity. A lot of them walked over five miles to get there.

I hadn't thought a great deal about my educational experiences at Ozone, but before I left there a woman who owned a big house came to me and said, "People have been talking about what you've been doing here and you're going to graduate from college next year. Why don't you come and live here? I'm getting ready to retire and I'll give you my house if you'll come and start a program here."

Somehow this experience in Ozone didn't stand out in my mind until much later, when I was trying to find education models through literature and visiting schools and utopian communities, and then I came back to this unanalyzed experience. I used to make notes on library cards, and whenever I'd refer to the Ozone idea I'd just use an "O" for Ozone, which represented to me not the method I've described—I didn't come to that until much later—but rootage, that is, it stood for real people. I could ask myself about an educational idea, "Would it work in Ozone?" as if I were asking, "Would it play in Peoria?" That was how I kept myself rooted all through the years I was studying. It was only much later, when I went to Denmark, that I suddenly realized this was more than a symbol of rootage and that I had some experiences I could build on.

I got involved in union activities during college. I had gone out to talk to some workers in a local woolen mill, and although I didn't know about unions, I knew that the workers there were being mistreated. I talked to them about how they shouldn't have to put up with low wages and terrible conditions, and that they ought to do something about it. I really wasn't trying to organize a union, I was just attempting to get them to think about their situation at the mill. Unbeknownst to me at that time, any college student going out and talking to these people raised suspicion. The companies usually controlled the local ministers and politicians, and they undoubtedly had a stool pigeon at the plant. And there I was, someone who didn't fit in.

The head of the mill was John Edgerton, who used to be president of the Southern Manufacturers' Association. He organized the SMA because he believed the National Manufacturers' Association was communistic. When he found out I'd been talking to his workers, he went to the president of Cumberland University and denounced me for causing trouble. That sharpened the issue. I didn't do much with it then except that I kept on thinking about it.

Racism was easier for me to get a hold of than the economic system. Racism was a matter of not respecting people. It went against all my principles. Later I came to understand the class structure of society better, but back then I was interested in these things primarily on a personal basis.

The year I graduated, John Edgerton made a speech at the college. In it he said that a lot of outside agitators were coming into the South, coming into the plants, trying to stir up the people, trying to get them organized, to make demands on the company that would put it out of business and interfere with the profit system. He said, "When we, the manufacturers, in our judgment, see fit to pay people more, or change conditions, we will. But we won't tolerate interference from the workers, because we give them their livelihood, they owe everything they have to us."

That absolutely set me wild, my blood just boiled. That one statement, that contemptuous attitude, did as much as anything I'd read, or ever heard, to get me thinking. To hear Edgerton's statement was one of my most radicalizing experiences. It changed my life and moved me light-years ahead of just basing ideas on loving individual people. It started me thinking about classes of people and economic problems.

THE CHRISTIAN CENTURY
September 7, 1938

South Loses
Five Leaders

Death Removes Prominent Men Symbolic of Forces Active in Section for Good or Ill

(Correspondence from the New South)

NASHVILLE, Aug. 25.—Five leaders in the southland who have recently died symbolized the forces that are leading public opinion in "the nation's number one social problem." John E. Edgerton was president of the National Manufacturers' Association for more than a decade, of the Tennessee body for more than two decades and was both initiator and president of a southeastern manufacturers association organized especially to fight the NRA and the New Deal. He was an ardent churchman, held prayer meetings in his factory (on the employees' time) and commended the practice to his fellow employers as contributing to worker efficiency. He was an equally ardent supporter of the old laissez faire economics, opposed in militant fashion practically every piece of social legislation proposed in the 25 years of his industrial leadership, declared he had, as an employer, no obligation to pay a living wage but that as a churchman he did have an obligation to care for those who did not receive it.

25

Up to that time I had just done general reading. Cumberland's library had a good selection of works written up to 1900, but nothing much beyond, except in English literature. In the latter, however, there were some references to Marx, some Fabian socialist writings, books about utopian communities such as the Shakers and books about populist organizations. And, for some reason, one of my professors loaned me a book on Eugene Debs.

The year after I left Cumberland (1928–1929), I worked as state secretary for the Student YMCA. I wanted to get my thinking clear, so I roamed the mountains, hitchhiked around, talked to and worked with people. I had grown up in a religious world and was trying to get beyond that to understand the broader economic, cultural, and social contexts in which things happened. I wanted to find ways to work with people in co-ops and learn more about the miners' union. I also visited what remained of several utopian communities founded in the Cumberland Mountains in the 1880s, such as the Rugby and Ruskin colonies. I wanted to experience firsthand things I'd read about but hadn't shown much interest in before.

I spent a lot of time at Rugby, which had been a utopian colony started by the Englishman Thomas Hughes in 1880. It lasted only two years. Some of the old-timers were still there and I got to know them. Will Walton, the son of the original surveyor, took me to his home, where I explored his attic for all kinds of magazines and other remnants of the community.

During that year after leaving Cumberland, I was trying to synthesize my understanding of the nature of society and my own values and beliefs. The contradiction was so strong I couldn't get the two together. I was no longer seeking to work solely from a religious or a personal basis. I couldn't improve on what my mother said when I once asked her what all this theology stuff was about. She had said, "Don't worry about that, all you need to do is love people." I didn't have to understand theology, heaven and hell, any of those things. They all just faded out of my mind. But I did have love nailed down. My mother showed me the difference between the preachers and the churches, and Christian values. She showed me how to avoid mistaking the church for religion.

From Jesus and the prophets I had learned about the importance of loving people, the importance of being a revolutionary, standing up and saying that this system is unjust. Jesus to me was a person who had the vision to project a society in which people would be equally respected, in which property would be shared; he was a person who said you have to love your enemies, you have to love the people who despise you.

Those were the teachings and actions that I wanted to incorporate into my life. I wanted and still want to see a world in which people can be equal, where people give their property to be held in common if they can't make personal use of it. I'd like to see a world where you could really love your enemies, where you could really care for people, a humane world. I don't live in that kind of a world, but I want to help create one like it.

Christ is one of the few examples of someone who simply did what he believed in and paid the price and would have done it again if he'd lived. That's why he was killed. When he was told, "You can't do this anymore, we're going to kill you," he kept on doing it. I learned from Jesus the risks you've got to take if you're going to act. To make life worth living you have to believe in those things that will bring about justice in society, and be willing to die for them. Now, Jesus was willing to die for what he believed in. I accept that as axiomatic: something worth struggling for is worth dying for.

In those days, I was trying to understand how love can exist in a society that exploits people. I had already come to understand the violence of poverty. Some of my friends—pacifists and others—didn't seem to understand that. I've had a running argument all my life with people who talk about lesser forms of violence, personal violence such as armed theft and assault, as if they were the only forms of violence. I didn't have to work out theories about the violence of poverty, because I had been close to it all my life. The violence of poverty destroys families, twists minds, hurts in many ways beyond the pain of hunger.

There is another kind of violence that supports the violence of poverty, and that is institutionally sanctioned violence. We live in a violent society, a violent world; that is, a world in which force is a vital mechanism used to keep the economic and social system intact. We have laws that are backed up by a police force; and the state, when the police force can't control defiance, is backed up by armies. The laws of the land are supported by the use of violence; that is, the use of physical force to make people obey the law. This is the premise you have to start with. If you oppose things in that system, then all those powers of violence can be used to force you into line. If you're trying to change things, first you have to know that violence can be used against you, and second, you have to know what strategies to use in order to change the system, given that situation.

If you have freedom of speech, if you have the opportunity to discuss things in a nonviolent way, as long as you keep from coming into conflict with that violence, you will have opportunities to maneuver.

As part of a minority group, you shouldn't think in terms of playing the game by their rules, of using violence to get what you want, even if you don't have any philosophical problem with it. On a level of strategy it's quite obvious that you have to try and work out ways of creating social change which avoid coming into violent conflict with that power of the state.

Education per se, just the idea of education, is nonviolent. This doesn't mean that you have a pacifist's philosophical commitment to nonviolence, but that nonviolence is the only commonsense approach under the circumstances. It's obvious that if you're going to try to bring about change, you must have what we call civil liberties, including freedom of speech, in order to function nonviolently. That's why it's so important to protect the right to effect change nonviolently, and you protect it and keep it intact by exercising your rights.

I was thinking about these things in the late 1920s, trying to figure out a way to deal with inhumanity, injustice and the violence of poverty. I knew that they were inherent in our capitalist system. By 1929 I was no longer interested in organized religion. I knew my values. They came from religion and my family. What I was interested in was social responsibility, so I started exploring politics, sociology, many different fields. I didn't have any radical commitments. I didn't know any socialists or Communists, that wasn't part of my heritage, but I began to read everything I could find about solving human problems.

When I was running the daily vacation Bible schools I sometimes stayed with a returned missionary who had been pensioned off to work in one of the small rural churches in the mountains. I used to carry around an anthology of English literature, and once he saw me reading poetry. He asked me which poets I particularly liked, and I told him Shelley had written one of my favorite poems. The minister took out his little leather-bound volume of Shelley's verses and gave it to me. I carried it around in a knapsack for years, and it's still one of my treasures.

The poems that especially interested me were *Queen Mab* and *Prometheus Unbound*. *Queen Mab* is a fairy tale, a liberating story that talks about life in all its forms:

> Commerce has set the mark of selfishness,
> The signet of its all-enslaving power,
> Upon a shining ore, and called it gold;
> Before whose image bow the vulgar great,
> The vainly rich, the miserable proud,
> The mob of peasants, nobles, priests, and kings,
> And with blind feelings reverence the power
> That grinds them to the dust of misery.
> But in the temple of their hireling hearts
> Gold is a living god, and rules in scorn
> All earthly things but virtue.

Shelley meant a lot to me when I was in college because I was beginning to get very cynical about religious people and about officials—mayors and other bureaucrats and politicians. I discovered a lot about such people and how they operated, and I found out what hypocrites they were when I worked as a store clerk while in high school. I learned how the town fathers were one thing on Sunday, and the rest of the week they were doing all kinds of chiseling.

I was getting very discouraged, and from my limited background I couldn't see anything to keep myself going. When I ran into Shelley I found someone who felt the way I did, and at the same time he challenged me. I remember from *Prometheus Unbound*:

> The soul of man, like unextinguished fire,
> Yet burns towards heaven with fierce reproach, and doubt,
> And lamentation, and reluctant prayer,
> Hurling up insurrection, which might make
> Our antique empire insecure, though built
> On eldest faith, and hell's coeval, fear;

For me Shelley was fighting against evil, pained by the suffering he saw and defying the world as an individual. He didn't think

29

much about groups and organizing. Of course he knew about the problems of developing community. His father-in-law, William Godwin, Mary Shelley's father, led discussions about the obligations of the individual in a socially responsible community. In a way, Shelley was a socialist in his thinking, but he didn't consider doing anything about it: he was a fiery young fellow who was saying, "I'm going to live my own life, I'm going to be independent." That was what I wanted to do and be.

At the time I needed to have something that made me say, "I'm going to do what I'm going to do. I'm going to live my own life my own way regardless of opposition or what people think of me." In that way Shelley played a role apart from anything else in my life. He symbolized to me the strength you can get from your beliefs. If I hadn't gone beyond that, though, I would have become an intolerant dogmatist.

It was the rage in his work that I took to, not just the anger. Rage wouldn't disappear as long as there was any injustice left anywhere. Shelley had a metaphysical feeling, not just simple anger, and he had dreams for a world in which there wouldn't be a need for rage.

At that point in my life I was disillusioned, and he gave me the strength so that I could say, "I'm not going to fit into the system. I don't care whether I ever graduate from college. I don't care what happens to me, I'm going to live my life according to my beliefs."

During the time I was at Cumberland University and in the year I wandered about the mountains, I began moving very fast. I was trying to go beyond my provincialism. I took a good hard look at utopian communes, which appealed to me because of their spiritual, religious and economic background. After I visited many of them over two or three years, I decided they were not close enough to what I wanted. They had withdrawn from the larger society and had only demonstrated what you can do if you withdraw. They don't demonstrate what you can do to change society. So I discarded utopian communities as escapist.

That's where I changed and became philosophically a socialist. I understood that you couldn't act alone, and that you couldn't withdraw into a utopian community. To deal with injustice you had to act in the world. You had to share what you knew.

Right after my adventures with Shelley and the utopians I explored Fabian socialism. I read Beatrice and Sidney Webb and came to understand that skilled people who believed in justice—economic justice as well as social and racial justice—could help lead the poor to equality. If I'd continued on my previous Shelley path, I'd have just been an isolated preacher crying in the wilderness. If I'd continued on the Fabian road, I'd have just been trying to do good for others. But soon I began to understand peoples' need to act for themselves, and I also started to read about the problems I was working on. That was a little later, while I was at Union Theological Seminary in New York, in 1929. It was then that I joined the Socialist party. Philosophically, I was ready to take a position against the capitalist system. That's when I decided the system wasn't for me. All my background exploring helped me make that decision. Socialism seemed to me the only way to deal with the problems as I saw them.

During my four or five years in the mountains my ideas began to crystallize. Several years later I wrote an essay that described my perception of the situation in Appalachia during the late 1920s:

For generations men and women have been coming to the Southern Mountains to help us. They have put hundreds of thousands of dollars into missionary work and schools. Much of this money was raised by the tales of "poor whites" who were 100% Americans. They have done for us all that philanthropy can do; all that can be done by those who have for those who have not. Yet look at us now. There has been advancement, of course, in some instances exceptional advancement, but as a whole, we are still "poor whites," waiting to be helped. It is now time to realize that this will always be true, unless we use our own resources; our intellectual resources within and material resources about us. We must discard our blind faith in help from powers that be—whether in manna from heaven, or Red Cross flour.

Missionaries have told us that our problems would be solved if we were converted (usually to some particular denomination). Schools have held out education as the solution to all our ills. Whether we want better homes, a more spiritual community, better community centers—whatever we want we must build on a solid economic foundation."

I still wasn't sure what to do to solve the problems that were on my mind. One day when I was visiting Rev. Nightingale, he told me to read *Our Economic Morality* (New York: Macmillan, 1929), by Harry F. Ward, a professor at Union Theological Seminary in New York. Ward had been to the Soviet Union and wrote about how socialism dealt with some of the problems of poverty and injustice:

The final clash between our current economic morality and the ethic of Jesus is over the nature of man. The capitalist economy rests on the hypothesis that man is a creature who prefers material comforts to moral values, who would rather have an increase in goods than in the quality of existence. The only future it can offer man is one in which he will get more conveniences but less freedom, justice, and fellowship. . . . The ethic of Jesus rejects this estimate of human nature; insists moreover that the very making of it is the negation of personality, whose essence lies in the making of choices and whose development consists in preferring moral satisfactions to material. . . . The central issue in the conflict between our current economic morality and the ethic of Jesus is this difference of judgment concerning the capacities of man.

After I read this book, Nightingale, pushing me, said, "Myles, you're never going to solve your problems. You don't know enough." And he was right. It was through his influence that I went to Union Theological Seminary in the fall of 1929 to try to find out how to get social justice and love together.

FOUR

Union Theological Seminary

Union Theological Seminary was considered a very radical place. I was accepted there because they had trouble getting students from the South. Union was trying to break away from the stereotype of all of its students being effete or intellectual. They were looking for people who had been active athletically or done community service or had work experience. I qualified on all counts, but I wasn't a typical seminary student, I didn't have the academic background. At that time the intellectual level at Union was extremely high and most of the students had strong academic backgrounds, were from the North, and hardly any of them were poor.

I'll never forget something that happened the first day I got there. Graham Lacey from Richmond, one of the few Southern Presbyterians at Union, arrived at school in a taxi. The rest of us had come by subway. He got out of his cab and he asked a person standing nearby, "Do you know where I can get a porter to take my bags to the dormitory?" That person was Henry Sloan Coffin, the president of the seminary, who said, "I'll take them for you," and without blinking he picked up Graham's baggage and carried it in for him. That was my first lesson at Union. Graham and I became good friends and later on he became quite a well-known Presbyterian minister.

Graham was the only aristocrat in the Southern crowd. John Thompson was an intellectual and Gordon Ross was a wonderful poet from the Ozark Mountains so we had three mountaineers and one aristocrat. I fit in in terms of being accepted, so I was very comfortable. I didn't have any illusions about my problems because I knew what a mediocre education I'd had and I knew what Union was. I kind of hesitated to go because it would be tough, and it was very tough, but thanks to one of my professors, Reinhold Niebuhr, and one or two other people there who were very friendly, I got along. Niebuhr, whom we all called Reinie, was so open and friendly that he asked me to join a seminar for advanced graduate students, although I had no qualifications. There were professors and priests in the class, even a newspaper editor. When he invited me, I said, "Well, Reinie, I don't know . . ." and he said, "No, I want you to be in it." So I went, and I couldn't understand a word. He assumed that you already knew the background of what he was saying, and without knowing any of that, it didn't make any sense. I sat there for one whole class, and although I didn't understand a thing, I thought maybe I'd catch on next time. During the break in the second class I said, "I just have to tell you I'm going to drop out. I'm not going to go back in because I can't understand anything you're saying. I'm not going to waste my time listening to you without understanding, because I can go over to the library and read something I can understand." And he said, "No, Myles, you understand." And I said, "I don't know what you're talking about at all, I'm not going to go back in."

By that time a circle of people had gathered around. Here was this famous professor and he was talking, so everyone wanted to listen. He said, "I don't understand this," and suddenly he turned to someone else and said, "You understand what I'm saying, don't you?" And this guy said, "Well, I'm having a little problem." He went around and asked, "Does anybody understand?" There wasn't a soul there who could say he understood what Niebuhr had been talking about. So finally he said to me, "Myles, you've got to stay. If you don't understand, something's wrong. You've got to go back in, because these people won't tell me the truth."

Later Reinie would ask me right in the middle of the class, "Myles, do you understand what I'm talking about?" I was his barometer. The others were ashamed to say they didn't understand. I had no pride. I was there to learn, and I wasn't even worried about grades or credit. All I wanted was to understand, to know.

I went to Union because I had problems reconciling my religious background with the economic conditions I saw in society. Reinie later wrote a book called *Moral Man and Immoral Society*, in which he talked about society being immoral, and about people being moral and how they can live in an immoral society, exactly my problem. I was moral and society was immoral. I wanted to see if I could get help on my ethical ideas. By that time I was also interested in world religions. All that I knew about them came from reading the Encyclopaedia Britannica when I was in college. I'd studied books that touched on other religions, but I'd never done a systematic examination. I also knew I'd be able to visit different places of worship.

Niebuhr was brought to Union partly because he had the experience of dealing with working-class people. He was interested in human problems as well as the theological and philosophical ones. He also had a brilliant mind that gave off sparks. He was young and radical and full of enthusiasm, in addition to being a stimulating teacher, speaker and explorer. Reinie was an active socialist, and in 1930, while I was at Union, he actually ran for the New York State Senate on the Socialist party ticket with Norman Thomas. That wasn't uncommon then, people were proud to be socialists and Communists.

I wasn't a socialist who was anti-Communist, but I couldn't be a Communist. My strong mountain background of independence prevents me from pledging in advance to do what someone else decides for me. I could never do it. The Socialist party was a philosophical concept, and that was my philosophical bent. This wasn't unusual at a time when people like Niebuhr and John Dewey were socialists.

If I hadn't gone to Union, my world would be much smaller. I wouldn't have gotten to know faculty and student social activists and become involved in all the issues I didn't know existed before I left Tennessee. Some of these people came from as far away as China. I remember in 1929 there were brilliant Chinese Communists studying at Columbia University. Their discussions about social change and revolution were analytically sophisticated and showed a conviction and patience that I hadn't known before. I used to eat them up and then go back to my room and read some more in order to understand what they were talking about.

I had discovered a big smorgasbord of ideas and activities to sample: I went to Catholic churches; synagogues; Muslim meetings. I attended workers' education classes and spent hours listening and discussing politics at Union Square, where Communists, anarchists and socialists gathered. I went to union halls and strike rallies. I wanted to learn all the things I could and test them against my beliefs and figure out if they would be useful when I went back to Tennessee.

Once I learned what unions stood for, I realized that they provided a way in which working people could begin to get control over their lives. In those days there was an organizing drive going on in the garment industry. The International Ladies' Garment Workers' Union was trying to organize in the sweatshops, but its leaders weren't permitted to enter them. It was similar to what went on years later, when organizers from the United Farm Workers weren't allowed into the fields to talk to workers. The ILGWU called a strike, but the only way they could notify the workers was to distribute leaflets when they changed shifts or went to lunch. Some of us from Union and Columbia University volunteered to help hand the leaflets out.

The day we went, the wind was blowing hard, and it was cold and rainy. The organizers knew that the cops would do their best to stop the leafleting. They told us that we might get arrested for littering or blocking traffic, and to be careful not to throw leaflets around and to stay off the street so the police wouldn't have any excuse to arrest us. If we did get arrested, the union would bail us out of jail.

I needed to hold the leaflets in such a way that I wouldn't drop them. Because of the cold my fingers were stiff, but I figured a way to push the leaflets out like a machine to the workers leaving the shops. I was doing pretty well until I saw a cop coming across the street, and I thought, "Uh-oh, here I go." When the cop got near, he just looked at me. I figured I had to do something, so I smiled at him. He said, "You can't hand those leaflets out here." I just pretended I didn't know who he was and acted as if I didn't know what he was up to. Smiling again, I said, "Oh yeah, you can hand them out anywhere if you're careful, but you've got to be very careful not to litter. It's against the law to litter. You've got to hold them tight so you don't drop any of them," and all the time I kept giving them out. "See, you hold them this way and push them out."

He just stood there and looked at me. Finally, he shook his head and walked back across the street, where there was another cop. He whispered to him and pointed to me, and then they crossed the street together. The first cop said to me, "Show him." So I did my song and dance for the second cop. They couldn't believe that I didn't know any better than to try to teach them how to hand out leaflets. I got about five minutes' mileage out of the second guy, and finally he said to me, "Look, I ain't talking about how you do it, I'm saying you can't do it. You can't hand them out here, it's illegal. I'm going to put you in jail if you don't stop."

"Well," I said, "I don't want to do anything illegal, that's why I hold them tight . . ." and the first cop said to the other one, "This guy's crazy, he doesn't understand what we're talking about." And they just walked off and never bothered me again. I kept yelling, "Hey, let me show you" to the first cop, and he would scratch his head and keep on walking back and forth. He let me pamphlet there all day.

Around that time in 1929 I joined a demonstration in Harlem against the intervention of the U.S. Marines in Nicaragua. It took place on 125th Street at around Seventh Avenue. (Because I didn't know New York then, I can't say exactly where it was.) I didn't care who had organized the demonstration—Communists, socialists or religious activists. I only knew I didn't like the idea of our bullying another country. Seeing all these people taking risks by standing up to show their beliefs, no matter how unpopular, moved me along in my social and political development.

Another specific event that helped shape my perspective while I was in New York was getting clobbered over the head by a mounted policeman at a May Day parade in 1929. That radicalized me considerably. I had a red Cumberland University football sweater on, and a cop came along and yelled, "Goddamn Bolshevik!" and whomp, he hit me right on top of my head with a club. I hurried back to my books to find out what a Bolshevik was.

At Union Theological Seminary there were many long discussions about pacifism and its relationship to socialism. I used to argue with people about why I couldn't be an absolute pacifist, because I thought that there might be times when it would be a lesser violence to have a revolution. You have to fit violent revolutions into the whole context of thinking about violence. Violence is relative. Sometimes a revolution can be a lesser form of violence if people are suffering intolerably under their currently entrenched rulers. There are many different types of violence: physical violence, mental violence, the kind of violence that causes babies to be born with brain damage because their mothers didn't have the proper food, the violence that suppresses people's expression of beliefs and ideas.

One of these discussions about greater or lesser violence involved J. B. Matthews, a former professor of Greek at Scarritt College in Nashville, Tennessee. He got kicked out of Scarritt for dancing with a black woman. He went to New York and became a very active socialist who worked for Norman Thomas. When I knew him, he was the secretary of the Fellowship of Reconciliation. The FOR is a pacifist antiwar organization that was started in England many years ago. JB came into the left faction of the Socialist party and was actually working in a collaborative way with some Communists. After that he got disillusioned with politics and became one of the leaders of the Consumers Union. Eventually he fought against union workers. I lost track of him for a while, and when I next heard of him, he had become a researcher for Martin Dies of the Dies Committee. He made lists of religious people who were suspected of being Communists, lists of hundreds or maybe even a thousand ministers, and presented them to the committee.

I was a member of the FOR on my own terms. At one of the meetings the members were talking about choosing between violence and nonviolence. By that time I knew that the problem was much more complicated than the way they were looking at it. I believed that it was a matter of determining what was the lesser violence, not choosing between violence and nonviolence. Most of the poor people in the world don't have that kind of choice. The people at this meeting were more privileged, and they could afford to take a theoretical stance. I was always needling them about their unrealistic position.

At that time, out in Texas, there was a black man accused of killing a white person. A lynch mob was ready to string him up, but the police officers intervened, jailing him so that he could be tried. When the mob came after him, the local police called in the National Guard, but the National Guard refused to shoot at the mob or protect the prisoner.

The only way they could have assured his safety was to use violence against their fellow men, and they would not. They were nonviolent. They refused to use violence to protect this black man. The mob took him out and lynched him. So I said, "Now, it's complicated, and all of us in the Fellowship are against lynching, we're against violence. These National Guardsmen were nonviolent, they refused to use violence against their fellow men. I think we ought to pass a resolution commending them for not using violence."

And they did!

I was just bowled over. I was sitting there, wondering if I should let it go by, and I thought, to hell with this. These are ministers and pacifist leaders, and it would probably be a good education for them.

Well, JB was supposed to be there at the meeting—he'd been away—and he came in late and asked to be brought up to date, at which point they told him about the resolution.

JB hadn't seen me (it was a big-sized crowd), so he asked, "Who made this resolution? I think I know who made it. . . . This is terrible! Don't you know what you've done? You realize what you've done? You've taken a position for lynching! You're saying you shouldn't protect people against lynching! We can't do that! We're against lynching, too!"

They rescinded the motion.

That's how I tried to point out the contradictions in their dogmatic pacifism.

Four years later, in 1933, I was involved in a strike in Wilder, Tennessee, in which Barney Graham, the president of the Wilder

United Mine Workers local, was almost certainly going to be killed. I was a good friend of his and was trying to find a way to save his life. I tried everything I knew—newspaper publicity, getting the ministers involved, getting to the governor of the state of Tennessee—and couldn't convince any of them to move against the professional killers brought in to murder Barney Graham, even though I had evidence that the same men had killed eleven people in a labor dispute in Illinois. I had photographs of them as well as their history, but I couldn't get anybody to help keep them from killing Barney Graham. Barney was one of those stubborn mountaineer union presidents and knew he was going to be killed, because that's what happened to people like him in those days. The union members knew he was going to be killed, too, and they were eager to do something about it. After all the things I'd done had failed, they wanted to use some direct action and said, "If we don't kill these guys, they'll kill Barney." I had to agree. Then they asked me, "Don't you think we ought to kill them?"

I was presented with a real dilemma: should the gun thugs be killed, or should the gun thugs kill Barney. It wasn't any choice as I saw it. Since the union members asked me, I had to deal with that problem. I couldn't say, "It's none of my business." It was my business, because I was as concerned about the problem as they were. I said, "Let's just talk it over and see what we're talking about. I don't mind seeing those gun thugs killed if that would be the end of it. They're going to kill a lot of people, but would that be the end of it? Do you kill two gun thugs and save Barney's life and there'd be no more to it, or would the killing of the gun thugs start a war and a lot of you'd be killed? To me that's the moral problem. When violence is used, somebody's going to be killed. The right thing to do is the lesser killing. How are we going to figure that out?"

They realized they'd start a war and a lot of people would get killed, and they finally decided not to kill the gun thugs. I didn't make the decision, I just pointed out the problems.

Right after I realized there were people in Wilder out to get Barney Graham, I went home and collapsed. I was practically in a coma, but before I went to bed I wrote a story for one of the the labor presses at that time, in which I predicted the death of Barney Graham. I named the people who would shoot him and sent photographs of the thugs. I had their history and all the evidence. I added that I'd send a telegram later to give the final details and make any necessary changes. Then I sent a copy of the article and pictures to Alva Taylor, who at that time was a professor in the divinity school at Vanderbilt University. Barney was shot a week later, and all I had to do was give the date. There wasn't a word I had to change.

Once, a few years after Barney Graham's death, the question of nonviolence came up at a meeting of pacifists. I told them the story and asked, "How would you resolve a problem like that? I condemned a man to die, instead of condemning two men to die. Who should have died? In my opinion the man who did die shouldn't have had to die. Did I do the right thing? What would you have done?"

They sat there for a long time and finally one of the ministers said, "Well, I wouldn't get in a situation like that."

I asked the rest of them, "Is that your position, that you'd stay away from the realities of life so you could be purists in your beliefs and not have to make decisions between violence and nonviolence?"

I couldn't get anybody in the room to say anything other than that they wouldn't get themselves in such a situation. I said, "That's just bald cowardice; somebody has to deal with problems like this. Certainly the miners in Wilder had to deal with it!"

Of course any person in their right mind would be for nonviolence over violence if it were a simple choice, but that's not the problem the world has to face.

Pacifism in the context of education is a different matter. You can't use force to put ideas in people's heads. Education must be nonviolent. I can't conceive of another type of education.

I know that any decent society has to be built on trust and love and the intelligent use of information and feelings. Education involves being able to practice those things as you struggle to build a decent society that can be nonviolent.

I did my last fighting when I was fifteen. Until then I fought all the time. I thought that was the way you defended yourself, and maybe it was—I came from a pretty rough environment. Once when I was boxing with a guy at school, I blackened his eye and we became friends. Some people thought we were good fighters and began to promote us for their own entertainment. During the course of our final match we beat the hell out of each other. We were both battered, and people were making technical judgments about who was the bloodiest, and I said, "Look, they're making fun of us; they're making us hurt each other for their own entertainment." I took my gloves off and told those people what I thought of them. I just decided violence wasn't for me. It wasn't a matter of philosophy, it just wasn't any use taking that punishment. I don't use or advocate violence, but that's not to say that I can't imagine situations in which violence is necessary.

I had access to books at Union, and I found out about Marx and Lenin. They gave me ways to think about society, and that became a maturing experience. I realized I had to understand Marx so I could understand some of the other things I was reading, such as Parrington's books on literature and Beard's history. I thought they were so true to my reality as I saw it that I wanted to understand better. I was reading other books at that time. There was a Danish writer, Martin Nexø, who wrote a trilogy about poverty and the development of workers organizations in Scandinavia. I liked what he said but didn't understand how he acquired those insights. Other books I read had a Marxian influence. That was the transition. I didn't suddenly decide to study Marx, I was just trying to grasp what I was already reading. Marx was always to me a way to understand something else. I was not so much interested in his conclusions, predictions and prophesies as I was in how you go about analyzing and envisioning society.

In those days I was still coming from an idealistic point of view rather than from an understanding of the social and material forces that brought about the class conflicts, the contradictions in society that made it necessary for you to know what was going on other than in your head. I thought there had to be some objective reality that I could understand. It wasn't that I was unaware of the existence of social and economic classes—I had known that all my life. The first time I read about classes in society was in Alexander Hamilton's *The Federalist Papers*. His discussion of classes was concerned with the problem of how to balance them. What I didn't understand was how the contradictions in society worked in relation to the forces around me and what I believed and what I wanted to do. I never looked at Marx as somebody who could tell me what to do, because I never thought anybody or any authority had that power.

For example, I would wonder why workers didn't organize. If

they really believed in this, why didn't they do it? I didn't have an understanding of their need for survival and their conflict between holding a job and taking action.

I was thinking about myself: I wasn't going to be bought; I wasn't going to be intimidated; but I didn't think clearly about the forces of society that influence people. I still thought that if you believe in something, you do it, but I was beginning to understand that anything really worth doing had to be done with other people, and to do it with other people you had to understand the social and economic forces. It didn't mean that you were less principled, but that you had to relate what you believed to the real situation. It helped me understand that you had to organize; you had to have masses of people; and that change couldn't be brought about just because somebody had made a red-hot speech and said, "Let's have a revolution!"

The radical mood of this country at that time was just as influential. It wasn't very Marxian but grew instead out of more idealistic principles; a tremendous number of people had religious motivation, for instance. We had an uncritical feeling that we could change the system, based partly on a lack of understanding of the power of capitalism, of how capitalism could rejuvenate itself and of how somebody like Franklin Roosevelt would force the capitalists to take some bitter pills and get themselves in control again. Those of us who supported Roosevelt didn't think we were backing a guy who would be carrying a bunch of pills around for the system. In doing it he did a lot a good things, but he had to have the forces of labor to do what he wanted to do. Most of us didn't see that far ahead. We were right about the kind of society we needed, but not about how to get there.

Marx accumulated information about working conditions and what made the system tick, and he gathered a lot of unglamorous, unidealistic facts. His studies and analysis gave me an understanding of the system, and it was this understanding that moved me away from individualism.

My next real learning came from reading Lenin on the strategy of change. I wasn't trying to be a Leninist: I was trying to find out what was in his writings that could be useful to me. Lenin helped me understand that the socialism of the Fabians, with its roots in the intellectual middle and upper classes, would never work, because the people have to win the revolution themselves before it's theirs. If it's given to them or if it's arrived at through compromise, then it's going to run on a compromise basis.

I came out of all this reading and thinking in 1929 with an operational knowledge, a way of analyzing which made it extremely clear to me that if I was to use education to play any role in changing society, I would have to work with that segment of society that had the power to change society.

It was a very simple matter to know that this segment was composed of working-class people. It didn't take any great creative thinking to come to the conclusion that Marx was right when he said that revolutionary change would come from the working class. So, instead of thinking about having an education program to change society by working with all of its segments, especially with the people in power, so that change would come from the top, I made a decision to work with people from the bottom, who could change society from the bottom. That is the basis on which I decided to concentrate on working people, many of whom were exploited doubly, by class and by race.

It made no sense, however, to work with poor people who had given up hope. Only people with hope will struggle. The people who are hopeless are grist for the fascist mill. Because they have no hope, they have nothing to build on. If people are in trouble, if people are suffering and exploited and want to get out from under the heel of oppression, if they have hope that it can be done, if they can see a path that leads to a solution, a path that makes sense to them and is consistent with their beliefs and their experience, then they'll move. But it must be a path that they've started clearing. They've got to know the direction in which they are going and have a general idea of the kind of society they'd like to have. If they don't have hope, they don't even look for a path. They look for somebody else to do it for them.

Another person I read in those days was John Dewey. He was, in the 1920s and 1930s, one of the few people who had progressive ideas about education. Somebody once wrote an article that said I was a disciple of his. This was during the first few years of Highlander. Of course I learned a lot from his writing and from the times we met later on. I wrote him a letter saying, "I want you to know I don't claim to be one of your disciples. I'm grateful for the things I've learned from you, and I'm delighted to say that I've learned these things from you, but I don't claim to be a disciple.

I take sole responsibility for my ideas. And they're my ideas, and I don't want you to be embarrassed by criticisms of me that imply you approve of my thoughts or actions."

I got a letter back from Dr. Dewey saying, "I'm so delighted to find that you don't claim to be a disciple. My enemies are bad enough, but my disciples are worse." He didn't want any more disciples, because when disciples started speaking in his name, they'd modify him to fit whatever they were trying to get across.

If an idea works in practice, it doesn't matter if it's just something that's copied verbatim out of somebody's teachings. That's fine. Or if it's something you invent. If it's a combination of those things, that's fine too. Whatever works for you is good. You don't have to try to make it fit anything but the situation you are dealing with.

In the end I have to face the fact that whatever I think, in my finite judgment, with my limited knowledge, is the right thing for me to do at that time. I have to be the final arbiter of my beliefs and actions, and I can't fall back and justify it by saying, "I'm a Marxist, I'm a Christian, I'm a technological expert, I'm an educator." I've got to say, "I, Myles Horton, take the full responsibility, with what I know, what I intuit, what I believe, what I guess, what I feel. I am making this decision, and I accept it as my responsibility. I can't blame anybody."

Taking responsibility for your beliefs takes many forms. In 1954 I was investigated by Senator James Eastland of Mississippi, who was on the Senate Internal Security Subcommittee, and I refused to answer questions about other people.

He said, "You can't do that, it's against the Constitution."

In essence I told him, "I'm not so sure about that, that's a debatable question, but if it is against the Constitution, if it is against the law, then that doesn't have any effect on what I'm going to do, because I'm going to do what my conscience and my judgment tell me is the right thing to do. There's absolutely nothing you can do about it. Nothing. The only thing you can do is put me in jail, kill me, but you can't make me do something that I don't want to do."

Ultimately, you've got to take the responsibility for your own decisions. It boils down to that.

FIVE

From Chicago to Denmark

I didn't go to Union Theological Seminary in New York with the intention of becoming a minister. I went to learn things that would be useful when I returned to the mountains. That was the same reason I went to the University of Chicago the next year.

I had been reading about conflict, trying to understand how fundamental change could develop through education in a situation of inequality. I wasn't interested in resolving conflicts that would leave the same people in control and the same people powerless. I discovered almost by accident sociological surveys and papers that hinted at how to deal with these problems, and that there were a number of people in the sociology department at the University of Chicago who were studying social change. Robert Park, who was a professor there, had the reputation of being one of the greatest sociologists in the country. So I went to Chicago in 1930 to see what I could learn from sociology about how to help people solve social conflicts and change society.

I spent my time at Chicago visiting around, reading and studying sociology, and finding out what people were doing to solve social and economic problems. I had a number of chances to talk with Jane Addams at Hull House, a settlement house for recent immigrants. I took classes with Robert Park and learned about group problem solving and conflict as a tool for learning. At this time I began to realize that learning which came from a group effort was superior to learning achieved through individual efforts. I also began to understand how to use conflict and contradictions to promote learning.

If the situation arises, as it frequently does, that people in a group have diametrically opposed views, my interest is not in resolving that specific problem but in using the problem to involve the whole group in a discussion of the issues. Conflict sharpens the discussion. When years later we were holding workshops at Highlander about strip mining, one person might have said, "Well, I don't see why we're horsing around here, the thing to do is get some dynamite and blow up the machinery," while others would say, "That's the wrong way to go at it, because we'd turn public opinion against us and we need the support of the people." I know this dichotomy is something that everybody in the room had thought about. George Bernard Shaw once said that you only begin to solve a problem when you have two people who passionately believe in something state opposite views. That way you bring the thing out in the open.

In a workshop, conflict gets the whole group involved. You don't even try to referee between two people. At this point the group takes over the discussion, since the problem being debated is everyone's problem. And when this happens, everyone discovers that the issue is not as simple as the two people have stated it, and a lot of the complications surface and get aired.

My ideas of using conflict positively instead of trying to resolve it and to use the conflict to move forward in terms of social change grew out of discussions with Robert Park, though Park and I dif-

47

fered. He was more concerned with reconciling conflicts, but he helped me understand what conflict is and how it works sociologically. I applied the knowledge in a different way, but I learned about it from him.

I didn't understand all of this in Chicago in 1930, but it made me think about analyzing conflict in group settings and analyzing the structure of groups. Still, I was frustrated. Neither Chicago nor Union provided me with any model of how to work in Appalachia with poor and working people.

One part of the academic training in the sociology department involved visiting various places where people were doing social work. A few students at a time would go down to Hull House together. Now Hull House was the settlement house started by Jane Addams in the late 1880s where poor and immigrant factory workers could come for education, health and cultural activities. She was concerned about the terrible lives led by factory workers. She had also been active early on in getting the Amalgamated Clothing Workers organized in Chicago. Jane Addams and Alice Hamilton, the mother of industrial medicine, worked together and were both there when it was my group's turn to visit Hull House.

They seated us at a big table and went around asking why we had come to visit. Almost all of us said we were interested in social work and the great things they were doing at Hull House and so on. When my turn came, I just said what was on my mind. "Well, I'm not really interested in what's going on here now, but I'm terribly interested in how the place got started, the early struggles and how you dealt with the problem when you were put in jail, and what happened when you were branded as Communists." They just passed by me as if I hadn't said anything. I hoped I hadn't hurt their feelings, because that was a tactless thing to say. A few minutes later, one of the waitresses came over to me and said, "Miss Addams wants you to come up and talk to her." I thought, "Well, she's going to tell me off." When I got up there she said, "Why did you say that?" I told her that I was trying to think through what to do and wanted to know how to get things started. She asked me right there what I had in mind. She said it sounded as if I wanted to start a rural settlement house like Hull House. I said, "No, no, if it could be like you had at the beginning here, fine, but I don't want it to be like it is now." She laughed and said,

"Maybe you'd better come down here when we have longer to talk," and she invited me back many times.

She was extremely helpful in getting me to think things out. I can remember one time when we talked about this business of democracy and I asked her, "Well, what do you think democracy means?" She said, "It means people have the right to make decisions. If there is a group of people sitting around a country store and there's a problem they're talking about, there are two ways to do it. They can go out and get some official to tell them what to do, or they can talk it out and discuss it themselves. Democracy is if they did it themselves." I asked her where she got that idea, and she said she heard it from her father, who was a friend of Abraham Lincoln. I told her I didn't think that was bad advice at all.

I learned a lot about social movements, the concepts of how organizations work, while I was at Chicago. I came to realize that things had to be done through organizations. I knew that people as individuals would remain powerless, but if they could get together in organizations, they could have power, provided they used their organizations instead of being used by them. I understood the need for organizations, but I was always afraid of what they did to people. I once wrote something about organizations, saying that they end up in structures and structures become permanent and most of them outlive their usefulness. Later this became important to me when I had to decide what my relationship to the Highlander Folk School should be. Institutions must be kept from becoming oppressive or useless or taking the place of the vitality and life of people. I was very concerned about that relationship of the individual to the organization.

Much later on, the historian Page Smith—I met him when he was a provost at one of the colleges at the University of California at Santa Cruz—and I were talking at a meeting about how people are influenced. Page said to the people there, "Maybe you don't know it, but Myles illustrates how people are part of a process of influencing people. He was influenced by Jane Addams, and Jane Addams' father was influenced by Lincoln, so Lincoln through her father influenced Jane Addams, and Jane Addams influenced Myles Horton, and Myles Horton influenced Martin Luther King." And somebody asked, "Is that true?" I said, "It's two-thirds true. I can vouch for the first two parts, but you'd have to ask Martin about the third." Page wrote an article two or three years ago in which he tells that story, but he substituted Rosa Parks for King and had her saying I was the first white person she ever trusted.

Through Jane Addams I not only got these ideas, but she gave me introductions to all the settlement house directors in the country. The women who ran them became very staunch supporters of Highlander. It meant a lot to me to have all these wonderful women backing us up.

I did learn a lot academically at Chicago, although I never got a degree. I stopped working for degrees before I got out of college. They threatened not to give me one at Cumberland because I had too many credits, but they weren't distributed properly. I had six extra credits and good grades, but they said, "You don't have a major or a minor in anything." And I didn't. It was their problem, not mine. I didn't care. They said I could never go on to graduate school, but I said I'd manage if I wanted to. Since I was president of the senior class, the idea of my not graduating caused them a little problem. They finally decided to let me graduate, but not because of anything I did about it.

Robert Park wanted me to be his assistant. He told me that if I would stay on and be his assistant I could get a doctorate, but I decided that in my work I wouldn't need one. What I still needed was more understanding of things. By that time I was a student activist. I was president of the University of Chicago Socialist Club and getting so involved in all kinds of things that I wanted to get a little perspective.

One night in Chicago my girlfriend and I went to a folk dance at a Danish Lutheran church, where I got to talking with two Danish-born ministers, Enok Mortensen and Aage Møller. I told them about my educational goals and how I was having trouble finding a model school. They suggested that what I had in mind was a Danish folk high school. These schools sounded so interesting that I read every book on the subject I could find in the university library, as well as in Robert Park's private library. However, I couldn't reconcile the contribution to the democratization of Denmark attributed to the folk schools with the explanations of how it was accomplished. I could not understand how the methods described could ever achieve the results claimed for these schools.

I decided the only way to find out would be to go to Denmark.

· · · ·

I left Chicago in 1931 and worked until the fall. Then I set off. When I got to Denmark, I lived with a family in Copenhagen and studied the language at Borups Folk High School. I started visiting other folk high schools and found that they took the form of the earlier schools I had read about, but less of the spirit. There was little discussion in class or informal interaction between teachers and students. The earlier schools, founded by Bishop Grundtvig, were part of the mid-nineteenth-century ferment. They sounded more relevant to my needs, so I began to seek out some older students and teachers.

I remember talking to one of the old directors, the son of a founding father of the folk schools, about their early history. He didn't understand that I was more concerned with knowing about the roots of the folk schools and their contribution to greater economic and social democracy in Denmark than with what they later developed into. There's much to learn from how things get started. You can't cut off the top of a tree and stick it in the ground somewhere and make it grow—you have to know about the roots. He kept telling me what I already knew from all the books I'd read. Finally I told him, "What you're talking about is what Dewey and a lot of other people talked about. That's not what I want to know."

His response was "Yes, I've been trying to put it in your language."

Immediately I knew why I hadn't been able to get at the roots. I said to him, "Look, my question is limiting you: when you explain this in English, you have to use illustrations you think I'll understand, but I know enough Danish that if you talk slowly, and if you'll be patient with me, I can understand you."

He brightened up instantly, and I plunged right in, just struggling, and he called to his wife, "Brenda, bring tea, this young man speaks Danish!" As soon as he quit using my language and stopped restricting himself to what he thought I could understand, a whole new world opened up.

Talking to that old man in his language made Grundtvig's Living Word, which I had only learned about from reading, come alive.

I wanted to know more about the first schools and about the effects of Bishop Grundtvig's work. He proposed a School for Life to replace lifeless academic schooling. He believed the experience of the students could be awakened by a search for their roots in Danish history and Norse mythology. The people would find their identity not within themselves but in relationship with others. He also believed that through songs and poetry, students could grasp truths that might otherwise escape them, and that singing in unison was an effective way of inspiring people and bringing them closer together.

It was not only his educational ideas, but Bishop Grundtvig himself, that attracted me. I saw him as a rebel with prophetic insights; a champion and inspirer of the poor and voiceless. I imagined how the terrible economic depression which he experienced at the age of twenty-seven—about my age at the time—must have affected him, just as the depression then paralyzing the United States was affecting me.

Grundtvig's willingness to break with traditional wisdom was illustrated by the imagery in his hymns and poems, which were, contrary to the customs of the times, written in language the people could understand and enjoy. Nevertheless, he reflected his conservative times politically, even though he was moving in a democratic direction and had faith in the common people's ability to govern themselves.

The early schools could only be understood in their historical setting, which was marked by the end of absolute monarchy and the beginning of constitutional government. The social movements of farmers and laborers, and the cultural movement of folk songs and ballads were all part of the national revival. The folk high schools were shaped by and helped shape these movements.

The cooperative movement in Denmark was a direct outgrowth of the folk schools. They also influenced the rewriting of the constitution along more democratic lines and the growth of socialism in the cities. One of the first schools fought against a German cultural intrusion into Denmark.

All I lived and learned that year became a part of me. At the time, I noted some specifics that might be particularly useful in the future:

> Students and teachers living together
> Peer learning
> Group singing
> Freedom from state regulation
> Nonvocational education
> Freedom from examinations

Social interaction in nonformal setting
A highly motivating purpose
Clarity in what for and what against

The International People's College at Elsinore, where I was a student, and the Folk High School for Workers of Esbjerg were excellent examples of both the spirit and form of the earlier schools. They seemed to be breaking new ground, and were relevant to the needs of their time. The people did a lot of singing. They had made study circles and discussion part of the Living Word. Their directors were men of vision who adapted the traditional folk school idea: Peter Manniche saw the planet Earth as the International People's College campus, and he sought to build bridges among nations; Paul Hansen at his workers' school in Esbjerg was preparing students to live in a new society which they were helping to build and, in his words, to "enlighten and meet the workers where their greatest problems lie."

The successful adaptation of the Folk High School idea to the needs of a labor school suggested many possibilities for work of a similar nature in other countries. It was important for me to learn that the most desirable features of the older type of folk schools could be retained. In the transition they did not lose the emotional warmth made possible by intimate personal contact, nor did they discard the idea that each school should have a purpose or mission.

I rode from school to school on my bicycle and later made notes which I labeled "O" for Ozone, my symbol for reality:

Agricultural small-holders school near Odense: Here I found older and poorer students. They were better at questioning. After I went to bed, I got to thinking about mountains and asked, "Can an idea become organized and still live?"

Lingby, Dec. 2: More and more I feel the need to avoid all semblance of a training school.

Vraa: The job is to organize a school just well enough to get teachers and students together AND SEE THAT IT GETS NO BETTER OR-GANIZED.

If possible, the school should be on a farm where the scenery is beautiful and there is an opportunity for being alone.

Our fellow workers will be selected as students for their ability and direction of their interests. We will consult and share work. Effort will be made to keep them in the ranks of labor, but intelligently so.

Perry Horton working in Highlander garden. *Highlander.*

Go to strike situations and take the students, thus helping labor and education at the same time.

Students who go into industry will make it possible for us to have direct contact with the local labor.

The school will be for young men and women of the mountains and workers from the factories. Negroes would be among the students who will live in close personal contact with the teacher. Out of their experiential learning through living, working, and studying together could come an understanding of how to take their place intelligently in the changing world.

The school should help people broaden their outlook and acquire definite information by preserving, taking part in and analyzing situations of interest.

I wrote my last note in Copenhagen after I had gone to bed Christmas night in 1931:

I can't sleep, but there are dreams. What you must do is go back, get a simple place, move in and you are there. The situation is there. You start with this and let it grow. You know your goal. It will build its own structure and take its own form. You can go to school all your life, you'll never figure it out because you are trying to get an answer that can only come from the people in the life situation.

I still remember that night. It was the sweetest feeling, a five-year burden had rolled away, and I went back to sleep wondering why it had taken so long. It all seemed so clear and simple—the way to get started was to start. That Christmas night I had rediscovered Ozone.

SIX

The Beginnings of Highlander

I would like to see a school where young men and women will have close contact with teachers, will learn how to take their place intelligently in a changing world. In a few months, free from credits and examinations, utilizing only such methods as individual requirements called for . . . it is hoped that by a stimulating presentation of material and study of actual situations, the students will be able to make decisions for themselves and act on the basis of an enlightened judgment.

I wrote these words in 1931. I decided I didn't want to work on mass education, to do something that would cover the country. I wanted to use education in such a way that I could find out whether I was succeeding in achieving what I'd set out to do. The kind of education I started had to be manageable enough for me to know whether it was useful. Therefore, I decided to work with a small number of people. Now, if you're going to work with small groups and your aim is to change society, and you know that you need masses of people to accomplish that, you have to work with those people who can multiply what you do. It isn't a matter of having each one teach one. It's a matter of having a concept of education that is yeasty, one that will multiply itself. You have to think in terms of which small groups have the potential to multiply themselves and fundamentally change society.

Therefore, you can't have each individual go her or his own way and work separately. The people you deal with have to work with you in the name of a group, not for their own personal reasons. It was clear that you had to work with a union, a commune, a cooperative or a community organization; any kind of cohesive group that had a particular aim compatible with the philosophy of creating some form of democratic society.

I realized that if I was going to develop a program where people could multiply themselves, I needed to know what these people should learn to do. Clearly they had to learn to value their own experience, to analyze their own experience and to know how to make decisions.

Since I chose to work with poor, oppressed people, I had to take into consideration that they'd never been allowed to value their own experience; that they'd been told it was dirt and that only teachers and experts knew what was good for them.

I knew that it was necessary to do things in the opposite way, to draw out of people their experience, and help them value group experiences and learn from them. It was essential that people learned to make decisions on the basis of analyzing and trusting their own experience, and learning from that what was good and what was bad. So helping people with decision making was clearly necessary.

It also became clear that there had to be a place where people could learn how to make decisions by actually making real decisions. That's how you learn anything—by doing it. I believed then and still believe that you learn from your experience of doing something and from your analysis of that experience.

Institutions such as schools and universities are not places where poor people feel comfortable. They can't be expected to make decisions in the presence of experts, since they are used to having experts make decisions for them. Given that decision making is central, it became clear that I had to create a separate place where people could make decisions on things that mattered. They had never been allowed to make decisions on anything of importance in their own lives. In a factory you make decisions within the limits set by the boss. But here, at this new education center I dreamed of creating with other people, *they* were going to make decisions, the biggest decisions possible in that setup. They would make all the decisions having to do with their stay there, and what they were going to do when they got home.

Now I didn't know how to do all of this at the time, but I set out to find out how to make it work when I returned to Tennessee in the fall of 1932.

While I was at Union Theological Seminary and trying to think through what would later become Highlander, I talked about my ideas to everybody I thought would be interested—and some who weren't. Most of us were students of Reinhold Niebuhr.

One of the people I talked to in those Union days was Jim Dombrowski, a Southerner who grew up in Tampa, Florida, and went to Emory University, where he was a student leader and got a theological degree. He went to Union for another theological degree. After that he studied at Columbia, where he earned a doctorate. His thesis became a book called *Christian Socialism in America*. Jim wanted to go back to work in the South in some way. He was fascinated with the idea of Highlander although his background was purely city and academic. He was a warm, intelligent, sensitive human being.

I got to know other men and women in Niebuhr's class: one was King Gordon, whose father was the Canadian ambassador to England during Ramsay MacDonald's time; Ursula Keppel-Compton, who later became Ursula Niebuhr, was there too. I met Kay Bennett through her brother John, who was a professor at Union, and she had a classmate, Elizabeth Hawes, whose father was a Unitarian minister in Brookline, Massachussetts. Kay and Elizabeth, who was called Zilla by everyone, had been at Vassar together and campaigned for Al Smith, which was the most radical thing a college person could do at that time. They were young, bright women who had a lot of ideas.

Another classmate was John Thompson, a native of East Tennessee. John's father, a classical scholar, had educated him at home. John was so brilliant and knew so much that after only a year at a well-known Presbyterian college, he was given a degree with honors just to get rid of him. Despite his erudition he was a very humane person, and he wanted to work in the mountains where he'd come from. John hoped to become a minister, but he also wanted to work at what would later become Highlander.

Most people at Union Theological Seminary didn't understand the problems I wanted to work on. They didn't know the people in the mountains or mountain ways. Warren Wilson was one person who did, so I liked to talk with him. Harry Ward, Reinhold Niebuhr, Norman Thomas, Sidney Hillman and many others I talked with knew the problems of the cities, and they were generous, committed people who weren't afraid to take risks. I was working in my mind on how to deal with rural poverty, with land and mining and farming problems. Although these people didn't have specific answers for me, they had ideas that might be useful, and they helped me learn about strikes and organizing, about different people's struggles in the world and ways they went about solving them. I also learned how to get resources to support these struggles.

At Union the atmosphere was intellectual, the discussions very abstract, and I fell into the habit of conversation that was usual there. But then I had a completely different experience that was just as important, one which helped me understand how to speak to people. I spent some time that year working at the Worcester State Hospital on a training program for graduate students, especially theological students. Besides reading everything I could find on psychiatry and psychological analysis, I was put in charge of a ward. Before long, I was speaking hospitalese without even realizing it. One day a friend came with his girlfriend to take me to a house party with some other people. When I started talking my new language, the girlfriend started to get a little angry. "I'm not a doctor," she said, "and I'm not insane. Quit talking to me like that, I don't know what you're talking about."

It hit me like a sledgehammer and I disciplined myself from that minute on not to use any of the words I had picked up in the hospital. That was a wonderful lesson to learn: you can't talk a technical language that's only understood among certain people if you're going to be with the masses of people.

• • • •

All of us talked about setting up a school in the Appalachian Mountains, one of the poorest areas of the country. I'd bat ideas around with everyone, but none of these people had any roots in the mountains. I thought it would be advisable to find a place and bring in someone else who knew the region and the problems facing the people there before outsiders with no roots in the region came in. I said, "Let me go down and find somebody from the South, and once we get things started you can come down and we can all work together."

Before she came down, Zilla Hawes decided to go for a year to Brookwood Labor College in Katonah, New York, to learn about labor unions. Jim started raising money. All this happened before there was any Highlander, but they knew I would find a place because I was so determined to do it. I had made up my mind what part of the South I wanted to work in, but the form the school would take would have to grow out of the situation. All of us held on for three years, letting the idea cook.

When I returned from Denmark in the spring of 1932, I described my plans for a school to Niebuhr and he agreed to send out a fund-raising letter. One of the signers of this letter was Sherwood Eddy, then the international president of the YMCA, though he himself was a Christian Socialist. All the people who signed the letter were socialists. Sherwood was independently wealthy, and at that time he was involved in leading tours to the Soviet Union. Reinie told Sherwood he should give some money to me, but I hardly knew him. Jim Dombrowski knew him, though, and arranged a meeting.

I went to his office downtown and he said, "I'll take you to lunch and you can tell me what you want to talk to me about." On the way down, he said, "What is this business?" and I told him very briefly that I wanted to get some money for a school and later on he made a statement that somebody asked him if it was really true about his giving me one hundred dollars, which was big money for something that hadn't even started yet, and Sherwood said, "Yeah, but it's the first time I ever gave money to an idea walking down Broadway."

George S. Counts of Teachers College, Columbia, also signed the letter. He was one of the progressive educators who founded the American Federation of Teachers.

We collected about three hundred dollars from people like that.

THE SOUTHERN MOUNTAINS SCHOOL

TEMPORARY ADDRESS

Room 410
52 Vanderbilt Avenue
New York City

DIRECTOR
MYLES F. HORTON

May 27, 1932

We are writing you in behalf of an educational project which we believe merits the support of all who are interested in more effective labor leadership and action. Our project is the organization of a Southern Mountains School for the training of labor leaders in the southern industrial areas. The southern mountaineers who are being drawn into the coal and textile industries are completely lacking in understanding of the problems of industry and the necessities of labor organization. We believe that neither A. F. of L. nor Communist leadership is adequate to their needs. Our hope is to train *radical* labor leaders who will understand the need of both political and union strategy. Without local leadership a labor movement in the South is impossible. The need for such leadership becomes more urgent when it is realized that the individualistic outlook of the mountain people makes it hard for them to understand or accept leadership from without. Naturally, we will make the educational program as broad as possible and try to give the students and the community an understanding of the total problem of modern civilization.

We expect to begin very modestly with a budget of $3000. A young man in whom we have the greatest confidence is to be the leader of the school. Mr. Myles Horton has spent years preparing himself for this task. For the past year he has studied the methods of the Danish folk schools in Denmark. Mr. Horton is himself a product of the southern mountains and will understand the needs of the people as no outsider could.

The organization of the Southern Mountains School will follow, somewhat, along the lines of a Danish folk high school. A small group of workers, above 18 years of age will live with the teachers on a small farm where all will work, study and discuss together. Personal relations will play an important part. There will be a limited number of regular classes, but the smallness of the group will allow ample time for individual work based on the needs of the various students. The school proper is, however, of no great importance than the educational work to be carried on with the adult members of the community. The objective in general is to enable those who otherwise would have no educational advantages whatsoever to learn enough about themselves and society, to have something on which to base their decisions and actions whether in their own community or in an industrial situation into which they may be thrown.

This project will be carried out in the mountains of North Carolina, the exact location to be determined shortly. It will be necessary to have enough money to rent or buy a small mountain farm and to supply materials which can be made into furniture, and pay for books and food for the teachers. No one is to receive a salary. With the help of the community, in the form of labor and food, $3000 will launch the project and support it for the first year. An effort will be made to make the school more and more self supporting from year to year.

We are proposing to use education as one of the instruments for bringing about a new social order. Assuming that an individual can be integrated by having his interests aroused in a great cause in which he can lose himself, our problems—individual integration, relation of the individual to a new situation, and education for a socialistic society —become one.

We are anxious to secure pledges of support from $5 to $100 per year from a limited number of people who understand the needs of an educated radical labor leadership. If this project appeals to you, will you send your pledge or check to our treasurers, Mr. A. Albert MacLeod, The World Tomorrow, 52 Vanderbilt Avenue, New York City?

The names of the other members of the advisory committee who heartily endorse this project and who will be consulted by Mr. Horton in the development of his enterprise are listed below:

Sherwood Eddy	Sincerely yours,
Norman Thomas	REINHOLD NIEBUHR
Arthur L. Swifts	
George S. Counts	

Later in the summer I went to Atlanta to see Dr. Will Alexander, whom I had met at Union. He was the head of the Commission on Interracial Cooperation, and I thought he might be able to help me find someone to work with from the mountains. He suggested I get in touch with Don West, a young man from the Georgia mountains who had also been in Denmark the year before. Don was more or less a Christian Socialist who had been a theology student of Alva Taylor at Vanderbilt University. Don had already had an idea of starting a school for poor people in Appalachia before we met.

The two of us drove around East Tennessee in Don's old car. One night we ended up staying with Rev. Nightingale, who suggested we talk to Dr. Lilian Johnson. She wished to retire, and had a place in Grundy County near Monteagle that she wanted to turn over to someone interested in carrying on her community work. Dr. Johnson was a wonderful educated person, one of the first women in the South with a Ph.D., a former college president who had been a student of John Dewey before the turn of the century. Her place at Monteagle was a little bit elitist, but over the years she had worked out a program that tried to do good for the community. One of the leaders of the cooperative movement in America, she established a small agricultural co-op at Monteagle. She also brought two excellent teachers into the local schools. But that was as far as she went; unions, for instance, scared her. Anyway, she offered us the place on a trial basis for one year.

We had just made up the name "The Southern Mountains School" for our fund-raising letter. After we moved down to Tennessee, we kept the same name until Don and his wife, Connie, decided we needed a better one. I didn't care what we called it, so when Don or Connie came up with Highlander—I'm not sure which one of them thought of the name—I decided it was right. Although I had grown up using the term "mountain people," all the books at that time (John C. Campbell's *The Southern Highlander and His Homeland*, for instance) referred to the Southern mountains as the Southern highlands, and the people who lived there as highlanders.

We thought there would be other places like Highlander Folk School in every state within two or three years if we did a good job. We hadn't had any idea of coming to Highlander and staying there, or that it would be the only school in the region. At the start, Don had wanted to go to Georgia, but when Dr. Johnson

Highlander, 1953. Dr. Lilian Johnson (left), donor of original Mont-eagle site, facing Louise Thomas and Myles Horton. *Highlander*.

offered us her farm at Monteagle, that settled where we'd begin, and Don and I became codirectors.

Dr. Johnson was very critical of the school at first because she thought we were too radical. She was also unhappy because she believed that we were moving too fast for the community. She had given us a year's tenure, and after about six months she told us she wasn't sure she would renew our contract so I decided to start looking for another place in case we had to move. I had a friend in the Cumberland Mountains up near Kentucky who had a lot of land close to a town called Allardt. He was an old socialist named Joe Kelley Stockton. He and his wife, Kate Bradford Stockton, were mountain socialists who were considered atheists by lots of people who lived up there. They were great Tom Paine and Eugene Debs people. They offered us all the land we wanted so we'd have a place if we had to leave Monteagle.

About this time, friends from Union Theological Seminary started coming down, and from then on we shaped Highlander together. At first we didn't have a very clear-cut idea of how to go about organizing the school. I've always been afraid of overstructuring things because I've seen the spirit of organizations killed by rigidity. We were still toying with ideas about how to set up Highlander when Jim Dombrowski arrived and put his organizing skills to work. We didn't have a charter, we didn't have a board. Since Jim thought the plan out, we asked him to be head of the school, but Jim, like the rest of us, didn't believe in hierarchical structures. He called himself executive secretary instead of director or president in order to be recognized as a spokesman without being the dominant person. They thought I had to have a title because I was dealing with the educational program, so I became educational director. We took turns teaching different subjects, partly because we wanted to learn all these things and one of the best ways to do so is to teach them. This also made it possible for us to cover for each other whenever somebody was away recruiting new students, raising money or helping out striking workers.

John Thompson came down to Monteagle, but he still wanted to remain in a church situation. He worked at Highlander for a year before heading the religion department at the College of the Ozarks, in Clarksville, Arkansas. Later he became dean of the Rockefeller Chapel under Robert Hutchins at the University of

Chicago, but he was always on the Highlander board, and he returned to teach in the summers.

Except for John, who wrote poetry, none of us had done much writing other than theses. Jim Dombrowski is known for his oral research in Grundy County in the early days. He gathered information and collected some songs about the Coal Creek and Tracy City rebellion, in which the Knights of Labor took over the mines. He is also known as a collector of miners' songs.

After a year at Brookwood Labor College, Zilla Hawes came and headed up our work with labor unions.

Soon after Jim Dombrowski arrived at Highlander, he moved up to Allardt to set up the first work camp, where people quarried rocks for the school we were going to build there. He brought in workers from the mountains, as well as college students, professors and ministers, while I floated between Monteagle and Allardt. It was during this time that Don West decided Allardt was too far away from Georgia and that he would go down to a farm owned by his father to start another school. Don and I divided up what little we had—less than two hundred dollars, a sack of beans, some flour and books. He put his share in an old car and drove down to Georgia.

The rest of us actually started a program at Allardt, but then Dr. Johnson changed her mind and said we could stay on at Monteagle for another year.

The large house that Lilian Johnson had lived and worked in was both our community center and a residence for two teachers. The first organized activities we had were social evenings in which people of all ages from the community gathered to sing, play games and talk. We only had one student from outside the community for the first residential term for workers, but later he was joined by several other students.

We didn't have any scheduled classes during those first weeks. Then one day the wife of a neighboring farmer, in remarking about her unruly child, started a discussion about psychology with one of the students and a teacher who had stopped by her house. The next evening they continued the discussion at Highlander, and at the request of some of the neighbors and the residential students, we began our first class, a class in psychology.

Before long a class in cultural geography grew out of a community evening spent around the fire looking at pictures taken in Europe.

Dr. Lilian Johnson. *Highlander*.

Then, when the students and teachers came back with reports about a coal miner's strike they had just visited, it led to a class in economics. During that first winter we held four evening classes weekly, with an average attendance of twenty men and women ranging in age from eighteen to eighty.

The residential students attended the classes and had individual instruction in the use of source material, writing and public speaking. In addition, each one got involved in the community. One young woman who could play the piano started a girls' club that developed into a music class. So many children wanted lessons that piano playing was eventually integrated into the local school curriculum. Another student organized a dramatics club, and members produced plays about local situations for the whole community. A young man held educational meetings among the miners and relief workers in neighboring communities.

Out of this first year's experience there grew a program of community work, a residential program of short courses and weekend conferences, and extension work.

Although we accomplished some things by the end of that first year, we knew we really weren't reaching people the way we wanted to. The biggest stumbling block was that all of us at Highlander had academic backgrounds. We thought that the way we had learned and what we had learned could somehow be tailored to the needs of poor people, the working people of Appalachia. We tried unsuccessfully although as creatively as we could to adapt those things we knew, using slides about Scandinavia and a series of posters about the Soviet Union. We still thought our job was to give students information about what we thought would be good for them. Whenever they had a problem, we would try to figure out what in our bag of tricks would apply to that problem, and we would adapt it and make it fit the situation. We ended up doing what most people do when they come to a place like Appalachia: we saw problems that we thought we had the answers to, rather than seeing the problems and the answers that the people had themselves. That was our basic mistake. Once you understand that, you don't have to have answers, and you can open up new ways of doing things.

Another idea we didn't fully understand is that one of the best ways of educating people is to give them an experience that embodies what you are trying to teach. When you believe in a democratic society, you provide a setting for education that is democratic.

You believe in a cooperative society, so you give them opportunities to organize a cooperative. If you believe in people running their own unions, you let them run the school so that they can get the practice of running something.

We also found out that our talk about brotherhood and democracy and shared experiences was irrelevant to people in Grundy County in 1932. They were hungry. Their problems had to do with how to get some food in their bellies and how to get a doctor. We weren't equipped at all to deal with those problems, so we took a good look at ourselves and said, "What are we going to do? We're going to have to learn how people learn, and respect what they already know." That's when we finally understood that as long as we kept on learning, we could share that learning. When we stopped learning ourselves, then we could no longer help anyone.

In effect, we said, "We'll go back to school with the people and learn from them." Having these people teach us sounded right, but we were still caught up in formal thinking. We thought all we'd have to do was go to them and say, "What are your problems?" and they'd tell us. It was very naive of us to expect people who didn't know us to tell us what their problems were.

Questionnaires wouldn't work, either, because we would only get what the people thought we wanted. As we began to learn that, we found out that even if people did understand their problems, they didn't know how to express themselves in terms that had any relationship to anything we could do. We found out that people couldn't tell us what it was that they wanted us to do because they wanted to make us feel good. They thought it would be impolite to ask us to do something that we couldn't, and that it would hurt our feelings. Sometimes they didn't say anything at all.

We had to learn a new language. We'd joke about the fact that between us we had several foreign languages: I knew Danish, somebody else knew French and we had somebody who happened to know Greek, but the one language we lacked was a nonverbal one the people spoke. Since we didn't have the right language, we had to learn to observe people: to watch the way they related to each other, how they took care of their kids, and to be sensitive to their reactions to their experience.

We had to learn to watch people's eyes. When they talked, they'd look at each other, and when they answered a question, they'd look around and we finally realized they were setting us up. We just had to learn to watch. That's when we said, "We've got to learn a nonverbal language to be able to understand the people, because they're not going to put it in writing."

When I run a workshop these days, it's essential to see all the participants. I was working with a bunch of professors in a university in New Zealand not so long ago, and I said, "I can't see you." They were sitting in rows and one person said, "Well, that's all right," and I said, "It's not all right with me! I want to see the people I'm talking to." What I didn't tell them was why. I wanted to watch their expressions. I can't talk to people without being able to see their reactions to what's going on in a workshop. I can read people's reactions pretty well if I can see them.

When you ask a question in a workshop, people will look around to see who's going to answer it, or they'll defer to a person they consider a leader and never say a word themselves. There has been a lot written about this kind of nonverbal communication, but we had to rediscover it out of necessity. That was part of our going back to school and unlearning and relearning, and then learning to communicate with the people in Grundy County.

We also had to be careful about the things people simply didn't want us to know. People felt that their private business was their own. Some didn't want to talk about their religion. There wasn't a single family in the area that didn't have some member involved in making and selling liquor illegally, and people wouldn't talk about that because of their fear that the family member would be arrested. Some of the families had illegitimate children, and they weren't going to talk about that, either. There were always a lot of reasons for not talking, so we had to learn not to ask about certain things.

Once, I had to stop a visitor from pursuing a line of questioning. She wanted to be polite, so she asked a little girl who was visiting where her father was—I think the visitor also wondered if the girl was neglected. I knew her father was back in the woods making moonshine. The girl said, "I don't know," and the visitor asked, "You don't know where your father is?" The girl knew, but she wasn't going to tell!

It's very important that you understand the difference between your perception of what people's problems are and their perception of them. You shouldn't be trying to discover your perception of their perception. You must find a way to determine what their perception is. You can't do it by psychoanalyzing or being smart. You have to ask yourself what you know about their experience and cultural background that would help in understanding what they're saying. You need to know more about them than they know about themselves. This sounds like a paradox, but the reason they don't know themselves fully is that they haven't learned to analyze their experience and learn from it. When you help them to respect and learn from their own experience, they can know more about themselves than you do.

I learned another important lesson that first year at Monteagle. We bought a hundred-pound sack of beans and a bushel of whole wheat that we'd grind up and that's about all we'd eat. People were poor—we were all poor. One day I found a sack of potatoes on the front porch. I knew where those potatoes came from because there were only one or two people in the community who grew them, and I also knew they were very poor and had young children. My first reaction was "I can't keep these potatoes, I'll just take them back and tell them how much I appreciate it." But I got to thinking, "What a goddamned elitist person! You give your clothes to people, and you enjoy doing it, yet you would deny them the privilege of giving something to you."

The significance of all this was that it prepared me to be in the circle of learners and to respect other people's ideas. As well as giving my ideas, I was receiving ideas, and this helped convince people that I sincerely respected all they had to contribute.

People have to believe that you genuinely respect their ideas and that your involvement with them is not just an academic exercise. If I hadn't had these rather emotional, traumatic experiences of learning, to the point where it became a part of me, I couldn't have been natural about saying, "Look, you don't really appreciate how much you learn from your experience, and how valuable that is, because you've never been encouraged to believe it's important."

A little less than a year after the school opened, the first economic organization in the community was formed. A majority of the employed men were cutting what remained of a once valuable forest. The shoddy timber, called bugwood, was only used for its chemical content. The pay for this work was terrible, and the cutting was completely destroying what was left of the forest. A woodcutter who had calculated that he was making only two and a half cents per meal for each member of his family went to the other workers and told them, "It takes a sharp axe, a strong back and a weak mind to cut bugwood at seventy-five cents a day. Let's strike."

Soon the woods were deserted. The woodcutters held a moonlight meeting in front of the school and organized the Cumberland Mountain Workers' League. Within a week a majority of the adult population had vowed to be loyal to one another and to prevent the destruction of the forests and to better the condition of the local community by raising wages.

At a meeting the apparent contradiction between the community's support of the striking woodcutters and their interest in preserving the forests brought a comment from one of the strikers: "We really don't want to cut down the trees at all, but on the other hand, there isn't any other work to do. It looks strange to me that the government would be paying Conservation Corps boys a dollar a day for planting trees at the other end of the county while we are cutting them down around here for seventy-five cents a day."

Although the government program failed to make sense, the community had boundless faith in the government's willingness and ability to assist in a struggle against a rich and powerful corporation. After half a year of fruitless correspondence with various government agencies, a committee prepared to go to Washington with affidavits about impossible living conditions and instances of discrimination by the local public relief officials. Two thousand striking coal miners and textile workers in the area learned about the proposed trip and asked the committee to represent them too. They sent a letter to Frances Perkins, the secretary of labor, asking her for an appointment. When they arrived, they were informed that "the secretary of labor is in conference with important industrial leaders and cannot be expected to give her personal attention to every delegation of workers that comes to see her."

After three days of waiting, part of the time without food, the woodcutters' committee returned home without having seen the secretary. They had gotten a severe but practical course in community problems.

Many of the people were discouraged, but others turned their attention to cooperatives. Fifteen men and women asked us to give a course on the history and organization of cooperatives, which they attended for two hours every day for two weeks. The only good farm in the community happened to be for sale at that time, and encouraged by a visiting government representative, the community members made a grant request to the Federal Emergency Relief Administration for money to finance a cooperative program. Not being certain the government aid would come through and anxious to start a part of the cooperative program immediately, the group made plans for a cannery. The men built a cooking vat and a large outdoor furnace. The state relief agency provided cans, and the group bought a sealer. Each family grew what vegetables their land would produce and brought them to the cannery. The canned food was divided according to the amount each family brought, with one seventh going to the elected manager for general expenses.

Finally, the Federal Emergency Relief Administration made a grant of $7,000 for purchasing land and equipment for a producer-consumer co-op; however, the president of the Southern States Industrial Council, John Edgerton, along with others who opposed any organization of workers, protested the grant award, saying that it would be used by the Highlander Folk School for the teaching of anti-American doctrines, and FERA withdrew the grant.

Still determined to experiment with producers' cooperatives, as well as to develop their buying club into a cooperative store, the members rented a plot of land and grew enough tomatoes for everyone in the co-op. The following summer they rented a larger plot and fully expected to grow and can surplus products for which they had already found a market, but a prolonged summer drought destroyed the entire crop and left the cooperative in debt.

The community leaders concluded that the natural resources of their own and numerous other mountain communities could not provide subsistence. On the other hand, the high national unemployment rate made it impossible to get jobs anywhere else, so they were forced to stay where they were.

From their recent experience they also assumed that the present form of government, local and national, could not be counted on to do anything that was objectionable to the owning class.

Their request for a cooperative grant resulted in a lining up of interest groups. The only organizations to side with them had been the labor unions. The support of organized labor, liberal ministers and professors had encouraged them in their efforts to better their conditions. They then concluded, somewhat uncritically, that by

Zilphia and Myles Horton, first and second from right. *Highlander.*
Emil Willimetz.

joining hands with such friends they could obtain immediate demands that would soon lead to placing the national government
under the control of the masses.

In effect, the community had swung from implicit faith in the
government, through a period of lifting itself by its boot straps, to
a romantic conception of radical political action. When that action
did not materialize, however, the pendulum began to settle somewhere between disillusionment and the expectation of a not-too-
distant fundamental change.

Highlander, the residential students and the community began
to concentrate on organizing the relief workers into labor unions.

All the WPA workers had been put on the lowest pay scale of $19.20 a month. A corrupt county relief administration, supported by an equally corrupt county political administration, made union organization a necessity. Eventually three Common Laborers' Union locals, a local of the American Federation of Teachers, and two locals of the United Mine Workers managed to improve working conditions and slightly increase wages in Grundy County.

In 1938, when Highlander and local county labor groups worked to replace the corrupt county politicians, we succeeded in electing a sheriff, three road commissioners, a county court clerk and a school superintendent.

At Highlander we continued to set aside an evening each week for a community gathering. Usually the programs were informal, consisting of singing and dancing and occasional discussions of social, economic and political problems. There were forums on war, the importance of defending and extending democracy against fascism, race problems, the social teachings of the Bible, old and modern Russia, social developments in Scandinavian countries, and the labor movement in the South.

Ralph Tefferteller, a Union graduate, had come down to join the Highlander staff in 1935, and he gave a big boost to the community gatherings when he started a square dance revival.

There was also a growing respect for local history. Jim Dombrowski began to collect stories. He got the old-timers to search about in their memories for stories of the early settlers and to recall their own experiences as striking miners back in the days of the Knights of Labor.

Although a cultural program was one of our objectives from the beginning, it didn't really get going until Zilphia Johnson, a young woman from Paris, Arkansas, came as a student in 1935. Her father, Guy, owned a coal mine, and they lived in a big house on a hill. He was an outdoorsman and a hunter and a self-made geologist and engineer who invented some of his earliest machinery. Guy was a very creative person, and very strong. Zilphia was his pride and joy, and very much like him. One time he said to me, "Zilphia's so opinionated." I said, "Guy, you're opinionated, too." And he said, "No, I'm just determined." They were two of a kind.

Zilphia had been trained as a pianist since she was five years old. Two years before she came to Highlander, she won awards for top vocalist and top piano player in the state of Arkansas. Her parents were rightfully proud of her. But then she got mixed up with Claude Williams, a minister and friend of mine from Cumberland University. He was a conservative evangelist when I first knew him, and then he became an activist, a very radical Presbyterian minister—in fact, he was thrown out of the Presbyterian church. The charge was "being too active on behalf of one class." I remember writing a letter to the Presbyterian church, saying, "If you're going to kick people out of the ministry for being too active on behalf of one class, I've got a lot of recommendations for you."

Anyway, Claude was trying to organize the workers in Guy Johnson's mine for the Progressive Miners' Union. They had a contract with the United Mine Workers, but it was one of those sweetheart contracts, like a lot of the contracts at the time. That's when John L. Lewis was really a dictator. The Progressive Miners' Union was a socialist-led group that I used to work with sometimes on a volunteer basis. Zilphia got involved in this attempt to organize her dad's mine. Her father told her she had to stop going to Claude Williams' church, and if she didn't, he was going to throw her out of the house. She just ignored him, he disowned her, and some friends of mine sent her to Highlander.

I was always so busy while at Highlander that I barely saw Zilphia when she first came. Then the organizers in charge of a hosiery workers' strike at Daisy, Tennessee, asked the staff and students to come down to help. We stayed in the homes of strikers for a week, and she and I saw more of each other there than at Highlander. I had a chance to take a new look at her, and I really just fell in love.

I had been kind of shy when I was in grammar school, even in high school, and I didn't have good clothes and things like that. I couldn't buy books and do things other people did, so in a way I was kind of cut off. The girls would loan me their books—they were always friendly to me—but I was shy about this sort of thing. I wanted to make sure, before I made too much of an advance or got too involved emotionally, that the feelings were mutual.

Well, this time they were, and Zilphia and I got married a few months later. I was determined that she reunite with her family, because to me, someone without a family is bound to have problems. Mine was loving, and I was terribly disturbed about hers. I said, "We're going to go out there and see if we can work this thing out." And Zilphia said, "Guy said if you ever show up, he'll kill

Ralph Tefferteller (center, profile to camera) leading a square dance at neighbors' house. *Highlander.*

you." I said, "Well, I've been killed before." So we went to Arkansas. It was an awkward situation, but we finally achieved a little reconciliation.

Zilphia got interested in folk music and protest music and collecting oral history. She was in charge of drama at Highlander, staging outdoor plays for the community and dramas about labor struggles with the residential students. She became active all over the United States in leading singing for the National YWCA and labor organizations. Later on she adapted the church hymn "We Will Overcome" and taught it to labor groups all over the South. It had been brought to Highlander in the mid-1940s by members of a South Carolina CIO Food and Tobacco Workers Union who used it on their picket lines in 1945. This is her description of the strike in Daisy, Tennessee:

They asked us to come down and help them; make leaflets for their organization, to teach some songs and do recreation, and we went down. Washington's Birthday came along about that time, so they decided to have a parade and combine it with the things they were fighting for, because to them they were fighting for freedom, economic freedom. The children of the workers in the mill were in this parade; the school band was in it, and the ministers in the town who were sympathetic with the strikers were also in the parade. They were completely unarmed.

We were marching two-by-two with the children in the band. They marched past the mill and 400 machine gun bullets were fired into the midst of the group. A woman on the right of me was shot in the leg, and one on the left was shot in the ankle; and I looked around and the police had all disappeared. There had been about ten of them there. I looked down and there was a cop lying in the ditch, and I said, "What are you doing down there?" And he said, "Hell, lady, I got a wife and three kids!"

Well, in about five minutes a few of us stood up at the mill gates and sang "We shall not be moved, just like a tree planted by the water. . . ." And in ten minutes the marchers began to come out again from behind barns and garages and little stores that were around through the small town. And they stood there and WERE NOT MOVED and sang. And that's what won their organization.

In contrast to the community program, Highlander's residential term for adult workers was a more intensive period of study, lasting six weeks to two months. A majority of the students were sent by a union or cooperative, and they were expected to return better prepared to deal with the problems of their organizations. Usually they were poorly equipped to study, but eager to learn. Education almost inevitably meant academic training to them, so we made the courses somewhat formal, partly to meet their expectations. Yet most of our program was designed to encourage students to become involved in the community and to relate themselves to situations similar to the ones they would encounter after returning home. As part of their preparation they attended union meetings in neighboring towns and assisted in organizing campaigns in industrial communities.

In addition to the twice-yearly residence terms, there were informal weekend conferences at the school. Usually only a few people attended these conferences, but once, seventy people assembled from four states to discuss new methods of workers' education. At gatherings of this type, much of the time was given to singing, outdoor games and hiking on the mountain.

The regular staff members spent part of their time in the field as union organizers and in outreach programs. Many of these field contacts involved working with former students in their own communities and organizations. Our staff members were also available to help other schools organized by unions for the training of their members.

During those early years the community took part in all phases of the Highlander program, and this common interest created a spirit of solidarity that was put to the test several times. When the school had been in existence only a few months, there was strong evidence that the officials of a mining company and a hosiery mill, whose workers had been helped in a strike by staff members and students, had jointly hired a man to dynamite Highlander. The neighbors volunteered to help guard the school day and night for several weeks. Two years later, people from the community stood guard when the press reported that a group of delegates from a state convention of the American Legion, meeting two miles away at Monteagle, threatened to march on the school.

Sometime after this threat, the chairman of the Chattanooga Americanization Committee of the American Legion tried to discredit Highlander. Immediately a vigorous defense was made in a public statement signed by most of the people in the community. The Chattanooga Central Labor Union joined the local protest with a resolution "condemning such attacks on the Highlander Folk School as an indirect attack on the Chattanooga labor movement and the organized labor movement in general."

I used to express a lot of anger, and I found out that it cut me off from people I wanted to work with, because the majority of them didn't have that anger. Most were victimized by the system, unaware of how badly they were exploited, and consequently they felt no rage. Until people feel exploited and able to do something about it, they are not going to make structural changes. The number of people who are angry is not big enough to bring about social change. So, I said to myself, "I've got to find a way to work with people who should be angry but aren't. And, if I turn them off by saying, 'We've got to do this now, I can't stand it any longer,' and make it too much of a personal thing, then I'm not going to be able to make a contribution to any change. Somehow I'm going to have to channel my anger and my frustrations in such a way that I can deal with the people I want to help."

I had to learn that my anger didn't communicate to people what I wanted to communicate. It seemed to them that I was a frustrated liberal who wanted to get on in life and couldn't make it. They felt that I was taking it out on the system, which wasn't what I was doing at all. It wasn't easy to get to the place where I didn't scare people away with my determination to change a system that I believed to be wrong and unjust, but I tried my best to avoid sounding like an evangelist.

I had to turn my anger into a slow burning fire, instead of a consuming fire. You don't want the fire to go out—you never let it go out—and if it ever gets weak, you stoke it, but you don't want it to burn you up. It keeps you going, but you subdue it, because you don't want to be destroyed by it.

When I talk about a slow burning fire, I mean a fire that is banked for the moment. All the fire it ever had is still there. I can uncover a little bit at a time, and if it flames up too high, I can throw more ashes on it so it won't come up and burn me, and everybody around me. But I don't want to put it out, I want it to stay there. It's there, it could flare up, and there may be times when it should flare up. What you need is a good backlog going all the time.

In slavery days, in some places, the slave owners would say to the slaves, "You can have a Christmas as long as the backlog burns." If you have a big fireplace, you keep a huge log in the back that throws out the heat. Everything is built in front of it so that the heat can come out. The backlog is there, it slowly burns, it gets very hot and it makes better coals. You put a little wood in front of it, but it stays there and gives out heat.

You take ashes and bank it at night, and in the morning when you get up, the log is still red-hot. Then you take the ashes away and all you have to do is throw in some more wood. Now, the slaves would take a big log and haul it into the swamps and sink it. It'd be there all year soaking up water. At Christmastime they'd take an ox and pull that log out of the swamp and into the big fireplace as a backlog. It would last for two weeks because it was soaked in water. As long as that backlog was burning, they got a vacation.

The important lesson is that you've got to keep that anger inside you smoldering. You don't want to let it die out. Any time you want to build on it, to use it, you can make it burn very fast. Where that fire's smoldering, that fire's always there, always subject to revving up and getting going, but you're thinking in long terms now, you're not thinking in the short terms.

I had to come to grips with this when I realized that the capitalist system was more viable than I had thought. It had more ways of lasting than I had understood from my experiences in the Depression, when a lot of people, including me, thought that capitalism was on its last legs. When I finally found out it wasn't even limping, that Roosevelt's job was to make it work, and he did make it work, I realized that you had to slow down the fire, because you'd burn up the fuel and it would be over. That's when I started trying to calm myself down, and grasped that the revolution had to be built step by step, that it wasn't going to come as a great explosion automatically. It had to be made, or it wouldn't happen.

That's when I started saying, "Horton, get yourself together, get ready for the long haul and try to determine how you can live out this thing and make your life useful."

SEVEN

Rhythm

I used to travel all over the South recruiting students and trying to raise money for Highlander. Often I'd stay in hobo camps, where I'd spend hours with old Wobblies and hoboes. They taught me all I know about hoboing and catching freight trains. They also taught me a lot about how to teach. Once, I was in a hobo camp down near Mobile, or New Orleans. I had been hitchhiking in cars and trucks, and I needed to learn how to ride on freight trains, because they're better for long distances. I asked the people living in the camp about catching freights, and they told me, "Look, if you ride a freight train you're going to get killed, so we're going to have to teach you." And they actually simulated the whole experience. One of them would run along and be the train, and he'd make me keep pace with him: when he'd speed up, I'd speed up, when he'd slow down, I'd have to slow down. In other words, they taught me to synchronize my pace with the train until it was exactly the same. When a train pulled in, preparing to stop, they'd make me practice on it, because it wasn't dangerous then, and I couldn't get hurt. You have to put your hand up on the ladder, run a little bit to make sure that you're right with it—to feel that you're there—and then you just spring up. It's like taking another step, but this one is up, and you just flow into it. There's no jarring.

The hoboes taught me to get off the same way. You have to get off running the same speed as the train, and that's why it's harder. When you get on, it's easier to figure out how to synchronize, but when you get off, you've got to pace it in your mind so that you're going exactly the same speed as that train, or it will throw you under it or down on the ground. You visualize the pace in your mind, then you synchronize that with your steps so that you hit the ground with exactly the same speed. I know: during practice, I fell two or three times because I didn't get it right. Whenever I fell, they just kept on saying, "You've got to get the feel of it. You flow on the train, you flow off the train, just like water."

If you get on a train that's going faster than you are, it will swing your body around and your legs will flop out. It'll knock your hand grips loose and you'll fall under the train. They didn't have any trouble convincing me that I'd better learn this, because I'd seen people get thrown under the tracks. One guy got his legs cut off. You're learning for keeps, you're not taking a lesson for the fun of it, you're taking a lesson for your life.

There's an artistry to it all that most people don't understand. The hoboes would warn people, "Don't just think that anybody can catch a freight train, you can get off the freight train and get killed." They were very concerned about amateurs, especially at that time in the Depression when there were so many men and women riding freight trains. These experiences helped me think about the pace of social change and how to relate to it.

We had a flow of Wobblies at Highlander during the early years. They'd come up and ask me, "Is this the Highlander Folk School? Is Myles Horton here?" Since we had never set eyes on each other before, I began to get a sense of how word spreads, of how people tell each other about things that might be useful or interesting to them.

The best educational work at Highlander has always taken place when there is social movement. We've guessed right on two social movements—the labor movement in the 1930s and 1940s, and the civil rights movement in the 1950s and 1960s. During movement times, the people involved have the same problems and can go from one community to the next, start a conversation in one place and finish it in another.

Now we're in what I call an organizational period, which has limited objectives, doesn't spread very rapidly and has a lot of paid people and bureaucracy. It's completely different from what takes place when there is a social movement. During organization times you try to anticipate a social movement, and if it turns out that you've guessed right, then you'll be on the inside of a movement helping with the mobilization and strategies, instead of on the outside jumping on the bandwagon and never being an important part of it. You try to figure out what's going to happen so that you can position yourself in such a way as to become part of it: you do things in advance to prepare the groundwork for a larger movement. That way, you're built into it when the momentum begins. It's like learning to ride freight trains.

I had the benefit of guessing right about the coming of the civil rights movement. I have known the South very well throughout my life, and I've known people who could give me insights and information. One of the people who helped lay the groundwork for the Supreme Court school integration decision in 1954 (*Brown* v. *Board of Education*) was a South Carolina judge, J. Waities Waring, who was ostracized from South Carolina society for deciding in favor of opening primaries to black voters. Now I knew Judge Waring and had the benefit of talking with him and learning from him. At that time I also happened to know Thurgood Marshall, who was the chief lawyer for the NAACP when the *Brown* v. *Board of Education* decision was being decided. I also knew the other lawyers who worked with him. I could check my ideas with them and make educated guesses.

One of the things I wanted to do at Highlander was to hold workshops on the potential effects of school desegregation. An educated guess of mine was that the Supreme Court would decide in favor of integrated schools and that it would hand down its decision by June. In April I announced an integrated schools workshop for July. I recruited people, put out an announcement and got the Field Foundation to give us money for it. (We didn't need much, just a couple of thousand dollars to bring people to Highlander.) Everything was set up to take place a month after I had guessed the decision would be made. Everyone told me I would ruin Highlander's reputation if the court ruled against integration, but I figured if that happened, we could have a workshop saying why we were wrong and make something of that. I was perfectly willing to gamble on it.

I had to go up to Washington in the middle of May to see Estes Kefauver, who at that time was a senator from Tennessee, about something completely unrelated to the Supreme Court decision. When I got to his office he was out, but he had left a message with his secretary for me to come back at one o'clock. Since I didn't have anything else to do, I went out to buy a newspaper and sat on a bench in front of the Capitol to read for a while. When I finished the paper, I still had about an hour left. I looked across from where I was sitting and realized I was near the Supreme Court building. It didn't look as if there was a soul there, and I remember wondering if it was a holiday. I decided to walk over and take a look at the building just to kill time. I walked in and didn't see anyone, not even a policeman. I was wandering up and down looking at the things on the walls and thinking how eerie it was. Then, all at once, a door opened to the main chamber and people started rushing out. I spotted Thurgood Marshall, ran up to him and asked what was happening.

He shouted, "We won, we won," and then he asked me what I was doing there. "I've never seen you here before. How did you know to come right now?" Then we ran down to where they were handing out statements about the Brown decision. Thurgood got the first copy and I got the second. It's still in my files. I went back to Estes' office after that and had the privilege of being the first person to tell him about the decision.

Of course my presence in Washington on that particular day was a coincidence, but predicting the decision wasn't. I had enough knowledge and information to make an educated guess based on

85

talking with people involved in the case. It's important, however, to keep in mind that Highlander hasn't always guessed right about movements.

We decided at the beginning that the purpose of Highlander was to bring about social change in this country, and that there would be no discrimination, that we would deal equally with men, women, blacks and whites. Highlander was active in the civil rights movement educationally as it had been earlier in the beginnings of the industrial labor movement with the CIO. In both cases we benefited from the fact that nobody else was doing it openly. For some years before the civil rights movement started, Highlander had been the only publicly known integrated residential center in the South. When you realize it was illegal to have blacks and whites in the same school, illegal for blacks and whites to eat in the same restaurant, you can see why a school like Highlander, that believed in social equality, would have a monopoly on the business. Whenever blacks and whites and Native Americans and Chicanos and men and women got to Highlander, there could be no segregation, because we were too poor to segregate. We only had one bathroom for everybody. We couldn't have discriminated if we'd wanted to, because we couldn't afford it; and although we all believed that any kind of segregation was completely wrong, a lot of things that happened at Highlander happened not because we had some high-and-mighty philosophies and theories but out of a necessity, which is not a bad way to learn what works and what doesn't, and what's good and what's bad.

We started in 1932 trying to promote and work with an industrial union movement. There were few such unions at that time: the AFL was at a very low ebb, and the Communist trade unions had been liquidated. There was no organization to build on. We thought that what was needed in the South was a labor organization based on the old Wobbly idea of one big union for all workers instead of separate unions for skilled workers, because most workers were unskilled, and the industrial union idea was the only one that had a democratic potential.

We knew things were happening in the South. The Depression was on, but we thought the South would eventually be industrialized, so we wanted to get going and help people understand what would be happening so that workers would be prepared to go in and organize plants instead of going in to scab. We started working with the unemployed, a few textile workers, furniture workers, upholstery workers and people in the UMW, which was an industrial union.

When the CIO came along in 1935, Highlander was the only place that had connections with anybody in the South. We had developed ways of working with the new union people. There were always strikes and struggles going on in those days, and the opposition from industry was so enormous that we often had to work secretly at night. We knew workers outside the AFL and outside the Communist network (which was limited to Gastonia, North Carolina, and to Harlan, Kentucky,) and they knew other workers who were sympathetic to an industrial union. When the steel workers' organizing drive started in the South, the steel workers' officials didn't know us or anybody else in the region. An official of the Amalgamated Clothing Workers whom I'd met at a convention called me up to tell me they had decided to have a steel workers' campaign in the South. "We don't know anybody down there," he said. "Can you give us a list of eleven organizers?" Because we had already made connections, we could help them out.

By the time the CIO started moving in the South, we were already inside, and we stayed inside. Within two years Highlander became the official CIO educational training center for the entire South. Years later we anticipated the civil rights movement, not because we did an analysis and concluded there was going to be one, but because we found that with everything we tried, we'd get only so far before we'd run up against the playing off of blacks against whites. It was a barrier that stopped us from moving toward our goal of economic democracy. We began to pull together at Highlander the people we knew in the labor movement and outside; a few radicals and civil libertarians and ministers. There we started citizenship schools where blacks taught blacks to read so they could pass voter registration literacy tests. We had begun to build a network prior to the civil rights movement, but of course we didn't create the civil rights movement any more than we created the industrial union movement.

EIGHT

Working as an Organizer

In 1937 I organized textile workers in North Carolina and South Carolina for the Textile Workers Organizing Committee (TWOC). People there—black, white and Native American—were being exploited by the mill owners. Some of the workers asked me to come help them organize a textile mill in McColl, South Carolina. If you just pick a spot on the map and say, "This is the worst place, people here are treated worse and are in greater need than anywhere else, and they need organizing," it's very difficult, because there's nothing to build on. But if a spark exists there, you can go in and fan that spark and the fire will spread. The McColl textile workers who wanted to organize were a little more willing to gamble than the other people at the mill. They weren't the lowest paid, they weren't the black or Native Americans who had the dirtiest jobs and got only half of what the white people got; they were machinists, weavers, the semiskilled people who might be able to find another job. Basically, they had more self-respect. They knew they were being exploited, and they resented it more. Now those are people you build on. You spend time finding them, and you get them in the union. The workers with fewer skills at the bottom of the wage scale will often follow their lead, but you have to start with those people who have a little more security and self-confidence and help them organize the other workers. The lowest-paid people will join when they take courage from the other workers and begin to feel resentment and have hope of some success.

In South Carolina I had to find a key to the black workers. About 20 percent of the people in the mill were blacks, and at first they wouldn't talk to me. I didn't know if the reason was that I was white and a Southerner, or that they were afraid of the union. All I knew was that whenever I tried to start a conversation with them, they would walk away. I had to identify a spokesperson first, so I stopped trying until I had gotten a majority of the white people into the union. Incidentally, I didn't sign any of them up myself. I asked other workers to do that so it would be their union from the start. I'd collect the cards and count them, and keep them, but they got the signatures. People would come to me while I read in the shade of a tree and ask, "Can I sign one of these cards?" And I'd say, "Yeah, I don't have any here, but you go talk to so-and-so." I made them go through the other workers because I wanted them to relate to their own people. In a short while we got a majority of workers, but no black people. Finally I got to the place where I had to find a leader from the black community. After asking around, I learned that there was a man with a lot of influence who owned a beer joint.

I went to see him but he wasn't going to talk. His experience was that whites were racist, and that unions had sold people out. And here I was, knowing why blacks hadn't joined the union, and yet, I wanted them in the union. He wouldn't talk to me. He just pretended I wasn't there. Finally I said, "I'm going to tell you the situation. We have 80 percent of the white workers signed up in the union, but we don't have any black people, as you know. I want you to understand that we're going to have a union contract that protects all the members of the union. And, if the black people are in the union, that contract's going to cover them, but if they're not in the union, they won't be protected. I understand why you don't believe me, but you know they have no protection now. But, what you've got to think about is that maybe they'll be treated like anybody else and protected if they join the union, and I'm telling you the truth. One way you've got a gambler's chance of protection, the other way you get nothing. Think it over."

I told him, "I'll be sitting under this tree tomorrow, about two o'clock," and I walked out. At two o'clock the next day, he was there. He walked up and said, "Give me the cards." He probably still thought I was lying and that they might be sold out, but he was a gambler, and he took the gamble.

I told him we would be ready to go for a contract as soon as he got the cards signed. "And," I said, "you're going to have to help us get the best contract we can. We're going to have a strike, and we'll need unity and solid support." And he said, "You just tell us what you want us to do." The next day he had 100 percent of the black workers signed up. We struck the mill for a week, and the owner agreed to sign a contract.

When we went to the mill to negotiate the contract, the owner said to me and Paul Christopher, an organizer who knew a lot more about negotiating than I did, "You boys are Southerners. And I understand that, and I know us Northerners take a different look at these colored people. They're our boys, and we take care of them." Paul and I nodded, and he said, "Now, we've got to do something for them. They're going to expect some increase in pay." They were getting exactly half of what the whites were receiving. And he said, "You know, you're making me pay more for the whites, so we are going to give them something extra." Then Paul started to spill the beans, so I kicked him under the table. Then I looked the owner in the eyes and said, "Oh, I don't think so. I think they'll be all right. You don't have to do anything special for them."

"Well," he said, "I knew you'd feel that way, but I'm going to do it anyway." The contract he had signed called for a minimum wage that was double the black workers' current wages, a 100-percent increase. I said, "Now they're getting half of what the white workers are getting. Under the contract, everybody's going to get the minimum, so that'll be double what they're getting. I think they'll be satisfied with a 100-percent increase."

Suddenly he jumped up and cried, "What? We haven't been talking about the contract covering the colored workers." And I said, "No, no, we've been talking about union members. And they're all in the union. Every one of them." He said, "You mean it applies to them? Why, if I have to pay them what I pay the white people, I'll fire them." I said, "No you won't. The first one you fire, this plant goes down flat, just like it's been for the last week. You can't fire a single one of them." He had a heart attack right there in the office. Scared the hell out of us. I thought we had killed him. I ran out of the office and the superintendent called the ambulance and they hauled him off.

Well, he wasn't the only one who was surprised. The black people were just as taken aback as the owner, because they thought that if they got such a big wage increase, they'd be fired. The black workers knew they owed their employment to the fact that they were paid less. Only the black leader raised that question. I told him that they were going to be treated just like the rest of the union members. And he said, "Yeah, but that means that they are going to double their wages and they'll fire them." And I said, "If they do, we'll close the plant down."

I'd already dealt with the whites on this issue. By explaining to them, "If you don't treat everyone alike, they will play one color against the other," I was able to convince them. The white people were with me, it was the black people who were unsure. I just said to all of them, "This is the way it's going to be, because it's the only way you can have a strong union. And furthermore, we're going to meet together." In the South, when the blacks and whites were in the same union, they met separately. We were going to have one union, one meeting. I didn't try to sell the blacks on this joint meeting because I knew they wouldn't believe it possible and might be afraid of what would happen to them. We had a solid strike and closed that mill down. We wouldn't let trains run or any trucks make deliveries. We had men, women and children picnicking on the switch every time the trains tried to move the loaded boxcars.

The cowcatcher (one of those big iron extensions they used to have on the front of locomotives to move cows off the tracks) pushed against my leg one time. A lot of people, including babies, were sitting on the tracks, and I said to the engineer, "Roll over me, and then roll over the babies. They're next." The engineer blew his whistle and said, "I'm ordered to take this car out of here. I'll lose my job if I don't take it out." And I said, "You know these people will lose their lives if you do." And so he said, "Well, I've got to try." And I said, "Well, push a little harder." And he smothered a laugh and said, "I've done my duty," before he backed off. It really wasn't a serious situation. Because he was a union man, all we had to do was give him an excuse not to stop the strike.

Blacks were there on the tracks, too. There was solidarity all through the strike. People learned that they could work together.

On the first payday after the strike was settled, I had one of the most beautiful experiences I ever had in my life. I was sitting out a few yards from the line where the workers walked up to get paid. The blacks were paid on one side and the whites on the other, a real Jim Crow situation. The white workers, of course, rushed in. As they opened their paychecks, they were smiling and laughing, but the black workers hesitated. They thought they might get a dismissal notice, not an increase. Finally, one of them got up. He eased over to the window and was handed his pay slip. He took it and he walked over to where the other blacks were and opened it. Without a word everybody knew what was in it, a 100-percent increase in wages. The black workers all jumped up and ran together to get their pay envelopes.

Although we'd all been on the picket line together and they'd helped stop the trains, I'd never told the blacks, "You're going to get your increase and not be fired." I'd never made any promises except that all the members would be treated the same way. This was the first time that they could know I wasn't lying, so I was feeling good, and was kind of teary. I had my head down because I didn't want to show my tears. Then I looked up and saw the black workers walking toward me. They came over and one said, "Thank you." Everybody came by and thanked me, and before they got through I broke down and cried. I couldn't hold it in any longer.

Our next job was to announce that everybody was going to meet together. There wasn't any place big enough except the whites-only public school auditorium. We were told we couldn't use the public schools if black people were going to be there. "You know the law, it's against the law, you're a white person, you should know it's illegal."

That was in McColl, South Carolina, where there was a Klan meeting every week, where curfew was at sundown, and where, when the fire whistle blew, blacks ran to get in their wagons and cars, and if they weren't on their way by the time the whistle stopped, they were arrested. And I said, "Yeah, I understand it's illegal, but we've got to have a place to meet: we're going to meet in the school auditorium." They said, "Who's going to give you permission?" and I said, "We'll have to meet without permission." They said, "You can't do that, because we've locked it up." So I said to them, "Look, see this announcement? Tonight we're going to meet at the schoolhouse. All the union people are going to be there, and since we'll need to get inside, it would be better for you to unlock the door than have us take the door off. That's your choice." They opened it.

When I was asked to help unionize textile mills fifty miles away in Lumberton, North Carolina, I used some of the leaders in that strike in McColl to do the organizing. And years later a few of those same people were active in the civil rights movement. That was so far back, 1937 is a long time to carry over. However, many of the workers who came to Highlander from unions became leaders in the civil rights movement. In two places—Little Rock, Arkansas, and New Orleans—they were among the top leaders.

Once people took the position of working on the basis of equality in their union, they had to face a lot of opposition from their rank and file members, their families and the Klan. But it wasn't just the Klan, it was society in general that opposed them. The church people and the business people opposed them, so they had to be very strong. Actually, the Klan was less of a problem for them than were other community pressures. Their kids had to live with it; the union members went to church and the church was against them; they'd go to a bar and people that they drank with were against them; the newspapers were against them. They could deal with the Klan more easily than they could deal with the other pressures. But they had learned to deal with conflict and were fully aware that you can't make progress without pain. They had learned from experience how to buck the status quo.

I think that we may all be mixed up psychologically, but I don't think that we are going to solve our personal problems just by

Textile workers' strike, Lumberton, North Carolina, 1937. *Highlander*.

searching our souls or by getting a professional therapist to help us work out our internal, individual problems. I think these problems get resolved much faster in action, preferably in some kind of social movement. I have had the fortunate experience of being part of two movements: the industrial union movement in its early days and the civil rights movement. I saw something in those two movements which helped me understand that you don't have to work out your problems alone, one by one. When people get involved in a movement, they must take sides, and in the struggle, individual problems become less important or disappear altogether.

The same holds for resolving problems that grow out of social attitudes. For example, good people had been working for years on race relations, trying to change the antiblack feelings of white folks by changing their attitudes. Highlander's program was a social equality experience based on the belief that only action would change people's attitudes toward one another. Then, when the civil rights movement came along, these white people who were struggling with their souls got those souls right in a hurry. When a black person said to whites, "I'm not a nigger any longer and you are not going to treat me this way anymore," those whites had to act differently all at once and without the benefit of a long-drawn-out attitudinal change.

Thousands of people got swept up into the civil rights movement and underwent mass changes. Carl Rowan wrote a book in 1952 called *South of Freedom*, in which he said that there were only seven white people in the South who publicly advocated social equality. I stood up near the speaker's platform after the Selma march in 1965, and looked out over the audience. There were hundreds of whites, many of them Southerners. All those people didn't get changed one by one. They got changed because black people said they were not going to take it any longer. Blacks started moving, and they saved not only their own souls but some of ours as well.

NINE

Reading to Vote: The Citizenship Schools

Highlander had to break with the CIO in 1949. We had been their official education center for the South at the time they decided to kick out all the so-called left-wing unions in the late 1940s and early 1950s. Highlander was opposed to this attempt to prohibit Communists from holding union office.

I'd set up an educational program for the Packinghouse Workers Union and, beginning in 1951, they used Highlander for their training workshops. That union had one of the best programs of nondiscrimination of any union in the United States, so we had a lot of things in common. At their next convention Allan Haywood, who was the chief spokesperson for the CIO at the time, said that if the Packinghouse Workers union didn't put an anti-Communist clause in its bylaws, they would raid the union and break it up. It was pretty tough talk. Ralph Helstein, the president of the Packinghouse Workers, stood firm against that demand. He and I spent a week at Highlander talking the issue out. Ralph wanted to know what my position would be if the Packinghouse Workers decided to write an anti-Communist provision into their bylaws. I told him I'd resign as educational director. We had already refused to draft any such statement in 1950 at Highlander, and I wouldn't work for an organization that did. Ralph was the kind of person who wasn't afraid to stand up to the kind of challenge the CIO was making. We called their bluff and were the only union refusing to ban Communist officials that wasn't kicked out of the CIO.

Afterward, we lost a little of our interest in unions. Zilphia made a statement that her heart was no longer in singing for the CIO, because they had lost a lot of their principles. Her feelings were generally shared at Highlander, but we were still working with some unions, and although the national organization broke relations with us and asked the regional organizations to sever their contacts, the people in the South continued to work with Highlander. Many of the officials throughout the CIO were Highlander students, and several were more loyal to us than to their own organizations. So we were still doing some work with unions, but not nearly as much as before.

Even if we hadn't had that break with the CIO, we would have been working less with unions, because we had reached the place where there were sufficient numbers of them organized; we had trained enough people as educational directors, and we insisted that the unions enlist them to set up their own educational programs. We were phasing ourselves out of that program because we had always believed that if somebody else could do it, Highlander should do something else. We were trying to find a program, some area we should concentrate in.

We attempted to set up a liberal labor–farmer coalition, but that didn't work out. Although it did bring black and white farmers together—which was good in itself—we didn't achieve the overall goal we had aimed for.

We had made the decision to do something about racism—we

United Nations workshop, summer 1955. Septima Clark in front of blackboard, Anne Romasco to her left, Myles Horton in front of window, Rosa Parks and Esau Jenkins to his left. *Highlander. Coulson Studio.*

were having workshops with black and white people to figure out some answers—but we didn't know how to tackle the problem. The Highlander staff didn't approach it theoretically or intellectually, they just decided to get the people together and trust that the solution would arise from them.

We were in a stage with no clear-cut program, but we were beginning to have a lot of people coming to Highlander from Asia and Africa who couldn't find any other place in the South where they felt comfortable. This was getting us more and more interested in trying to work with people on an international level, not as a major program, but just another facet of Highlander. At this time Eleanor Roosevelt was looking for people to do unofficial support work for the United Nations, and we thought that might be a way to work with people in other countries. In 1955 we decided to have an exploratory workshop to see how interested people would be in using the United Nations volunteer organizations as a possible basis for relating to other countries. It was a shot in the dark.

As it turned out, we did a lot of analysis in that workshop, but it was analysis of the South, not the United Nations. We had economists there, political scientists, people connected with the United Nations, just trying to find out if there was an interest in that subject. The Highlander board had decided we had to deal with the problem of racism. It was on the basis of attempting to do something about racism that we were exploring these other possibilities and trying to find out from people themselves how we could go about it. We had set ourselves a goal, but we didn't have the slightest idea how to achieve it.

Some of the people who came to the UN workshops were from the Sea Islands of South Carolina, a chain running north and south of Charleston down into Georgia—little islands that were populated by the last group of slaves brought over to the United States before slave trading stopped. Many of the people there speak Gullah, a mixture of an African language and English. It's a little difficult to understand at first, but once you listen closely, you can figure it out.

The people who began coming to Highlander from the Sea Islands started talking about their problems. One man, Esau Jenkins, was an enterprising businessman from Johns Island who had a restaurant and a motel, and also ran a bus for people from the island who worked as domestics for the rich folks in Charleston. On the trips back and forth across the bridge, he would try to teach them to read well enough to pass the examination that was required for people to vote in South Carolina. But the trip was only thirty minutes long, too short to do much, and he also discovered that although a few people had passed the test, some were only memorizing the Constitution and not learning to read at all. Esau said that he wasn't interested in the United Nations, but he was concerned about getting teachers to help people learn to read and write, so that they could vote.

Another UN workshop participant, Septima Clark, got interested in Esau's program. She was a teacher from Charleston, South Carolina, who had taught on Johns Island and knew the situation there.

Now Highlander doesn't initiate programs; we help former students carry out the programs that they themselves ask us to help them with. I went down to Johns Island and was in and out for almost a year trying to figure out how to help Esau. I'd get acquainted by going fishing with the people. I'd spend the night with them, work with them on their farms and play with their children.

We weren't thinking of it primarily as a literacy program, because teaching people to read and write was only one step toward their becoming citizens and social activists. The immediate goal was getting the right to vote. Becoming literate was only a part of a larger process. We tried to fit literacy into a program that would be clear enough to be effective, and one the people could run themselves.

It didn't take long to learn that there was money available for literacy education in South Carolina. In fact, they couldn't spend the money they had. There was federal money and state money, there were literacy teachers on the payroll who hadn't had a student for years, so it wasn't a matter of money or teachers. Obviously we needed to look for something else. Once we put our minds to it it was easy to find out that all the past efforts at trying to teach the Johns Islanders to read and write were demeaning programs carried on by rather dominating, opinionated teachers who made the students feel so inferior that they didn't want to have anything to do with them. We were looking for the opposite approach, one that would be based on respect and make people feel as comfortable as possible in a new and difficult learning situation.

I knew from the early days of Highlander that you couldn't carry on an educational program with the kinds of people we were interested in working with until you could forget many of the things learned in college and start listening to the people themselves. I was trying to apply this "learning from the people" idea to the residents of the Sea Islands. As I got acquainted with them and acquired more understanding, it became quite simple. The only reason problems seem complicated is that you don't understand them well enough to make them simple. We needed to determine what the motivation would be, who could best facilitate learning and what would be the best learning environment.

Certainly the first people you want to avoid are certified teachers, because people with teaching experience would likely impose their schooling methodology on the students and be judgmental. We wanted someone who would care for and respect the learners, and who would not be threatening—which meant that the teacher should be black, like them.

Then we decided that it would be threatening to people to bring them into a formal schoolroom. Some unsuccessful literacy programs brought these people into the schools, where their grandchildren went and made them sit at desks so small that they couldn't get their legs under the tables. The children called the adults "daddy longlegs." We decided to find an old building of some kind where they'd be comfortable and feel at home, and since there was already a cooperative store on the island, we decided to use its back room for the school. We put in a potbellied stove, tables to write on (there were no desks) and some chairs.

Before the first Citizenship School started and the Highlander staff members were working on the idea, I did something that I've found very useful. I pretended that we had already started one of the schools in an informal place, with a nonjudgmental person in charge. The adults were there to learn to read so they could register and vote and perhaps learn other things they might want to know. I could just see these people in my mind's eye in an informal nonschool setting. Then I could see somebody who hadn't been a teacher before struggling along learning with them and working with them and drawing them out. I went through the next night and the next, and then I decided the students couldn't take it every night, so they would go twice a week. In almost the same way, I decided the program had to be condensed into a period short enough that they could see an end to it, say, the three-month period between crops, when they would have some leisure time on their hands. I figured out the length of the program primarily on the basis of the crops, not by intellectualizing about learning.

I made up a movie in my mind of what would happen during those three months, and when I'd see certain things going wrong in my mind's eye I'd re-edit the film or erase the movie and start over again. Then I replayed the film until I finally got most of the bugs out of it. After that I wondered how it would look if I ran the movie backward, and when I tried it I found some things I hadn't caught in running it forward. I'd sit by the hour and imagine all these things until I got it simple enough that I could throw away

Esau Jenkins, Myles Horton, Johns Island, 1950s. *Highlander*.

the excess baggage and all the things I'd done wrong. I did this because I don't think it's right to experiment with people when you can work out a hypothesis in your head.

When I thought I had it all worked out in my mind, Esau Jenkins and Septima Clark and I decided it was time to find a 'teacher.' Septima recommended her niece, Bernice Robinson. She had been to workshops at Highlander and had told us that if she could ever do anything for Highlander to let her know, but when we told her what we had in mind, she said, "Oh no, not that, I'm not a teacher." I told her, "That's exactly why you're going to do this. You know how to listen, and you respect the adults who want to vote."

Bernice was a black beautician. Compared to white beauticians, black beauticians had status in their own community. They had a higher-than-average education and, because they owned their own businesses, didn't depend upon whites for their incomes. We needed to build around black people who could stand up against white opposition, so black beauticians were terribly important.

That's how we started the initial class. Bernice and her fourteen students decided to call it a Citizenship School. The first thing Bernice put up on the wall for them eventually to learn to read was the United Nations Declaration of Human Rights. Since we were operating from the basis that these were adults with dignity, it was important to challenge them with something worthy of the attention and concern of an adult. Our objective was to help them understand that they could both play a role at home and help change the world.

Bernice began the first class in the back room of the cooperative store by saying, "I am not a teacher, we are here to learn together. You're going to teach me as much as I'm going to teach you." She had no textbooks or teacher's manuals. Her only materials were the UN Declaration of Human Rights, the state constitution and some materials for teaching schoolchildren which she quickly realized were too juvenile for mature adults.

Bernice and the students developed the curriculum day by day. They learned to write letters, order catalogs and fill out money orders. They made up stories about the vegetables they grew and the tools they used.

"They tell me a story," Mrs. Robinson told us, "a story which I write down, then they learn to read the story. It's their story in their words, and they are interested because it's theirs." She gave priority to their immediate interests so they could experience the usefulness and joy of learning.

At the beginning there was a problem over pencils. Many of the people in the class were in their sixties, and most of them were used to holding a plow or a hoe, or throwing out a fishing net. When they'd first hold a pencil, nine times out of ten they'd break it. The physical adjustment isn't easy. You could hear those pencils snapping all over the room. We decided right there that no teacher should ever show any concern about pencils, because that would be intimidating, but simply hand students another one and say there're plenty more. Because they had so many other obstacles to overcome, we tried to make unimportant things like that as insignificant as possible.

This first Citizenship School, which met twice a week for three months, grew from fourteen to thirty-seven students, and 80 percent of them graduated and got their certificates, that is, they registered to vote. People on the neighboring Edisto Island heard about the Citizenship School students' success in registering to vote and asked if they also could have a school. Although we hadn't thought beyond that first experimental class, we said, "All you have to do is find three people and a teacher. That's all. We'll furnish the pencils." They asked for some help, so Bernice went over and helped them set up their school. What we believed in was starting people on a path of group action. Along with becoming literate, they learned to organize, they learned to protest, they learned to demand their rights, because they also learned that you couldn't just read and write yourself into freedom. You had to fight for that and you had to do it as part of a group, not as an individual.

All the time Highlander was involved in the Citizenship School program, we insisted that while voter registration was a great goal, voting wouldn't do the job alone. We don't hold with those who say that you mustn't challenge people, that you have to be very cautious and tell them that if they take this first step, they'll win. That's an insulting thing to say to a person. We say, "That's the first step, but it's only the first step. If you're black, white folks aren't going to pay any attention to you even if you can vote. Sure, get in there and vote, but then you've got to demonstrate."

The idea was to stretch people's minds. One way we did that was to bring in visiting black activists from other places in the South to share their experiences with the students. We believed this all had to be done by black people for themselves in order for it to be educationally sound. By the time the Citizenship School students finished their classes, they knew that voting by itself was not enough. Even before the school was over they'd go to Charleston and demonstrate and make demands that public facilities be opened up for them. These were people who only a short time ago had believed they couldn't do anything. They felt confident now; they were being challenged; and most of all, they were forcing whites to treat them with respect.

When I first knew Septima Clark, she was a grade-school teacher with no significant experience in adult education. She had been an active member of the NAACP and was, in fact, fired because she refused to withdraw from this organization. So she wasn't an inactive person, but her experience wasn't the kind that would prepare her to work at a place like Highlander. She was recommended by the fact that she stood up and because she was already interested in the Sea Islands. At that time Highlander needed an approach to professional black people. Our record was with labor black people, not with teachers. Septima seemed to be the kind of person who could make a contribution along those lines. I had confidence that she would learn whatever else was needed.

It was a sign of her growth in understanding that this professional teacher agreed within two years of her arrival at Highlander that we should not use other professional teachers in the Citizenship Schools. Septima moved on to become the director of the integration workshops at Highlander, and then the director of the Citizenship School program, in which she was responsible for organizing and spreading the Citizenship Schools throughout the South.

As the first teacher, more than Septima or I or anybody else had done, Bernice Robinson developed the methods used by the Citizenship Schools. Never having been a teacher, she had to figure out how to accomplish this in her own way, and in doing it she hit on things that people now are doing in many different settings. Paulo Freire talks about it, people in Nicaragua are talking about it. Bernice was talking about those things then. She just got it from common sense, from her own intelligent analysis of the situation, from loving people and caring for them and, above all, from respecting people and dealing with them as they are.

Septima had selected Bernice. She backed Bernice. Then she took the Citizenship School idea and spread it all through the South. She played a major role not only at Highlander, as a workshop director, but later on as a Citizenship School director. Septima is honored as one of the outstanding women of the civil rights movement, along with Rosa Parks, Fannie Lou Hamer and Ella Baker. To take the benchmark from where she started and where she ended is the exciting part, because it shows her growth and development. Quite often her way of doing things wasn't my way of doing things. She was less interested in asking questions—I'd run a whole workshop and never do anything but ask questions. Septima relied on materials. I was trying to help people learn, and she was trying to teach people. The way I tried to help people learn was to share my interest in learning with them. She was doing the same thing —that was her way of learning—so she shared that with them. In that sense we were doing the same thing. Her approach was much more popular than mine. People want help. They don't want you to ask them a lot of questions.

Soon the Citizenship School program started island-hopping. We never brought anybody into that system from the outside. After it

Johns Island Citizenship School, 1957. At right, Alice Wine, one of the first people to register for a Citizenship School. *State Historical Society of Wisconsin.*

started island-hopping it began to move into other states and within two years it was growing by the hundreds. It was very spontaneous because it was so simple. Then Highlander was asked to help work out a program to orient more teachers. We found that by bringing twenty potential teachers at a time to Highlander for a residential training program and using Citizenship School teachers to train them we could use these new recruits to come back the next time as teachers for the next group. They were not only successful in helping people in their own communities learn to read and write and become citizens and learn to protest and demonstrate, but they got the dignity and satisfaction of training other people. Part of their job was to keep the process going.

We finally said, "Look, you don't need to come to Highlander if you're down in Louisiana. Get a place for the class to meet. You can do exactly what we did. You know who the teachers should be. You can do the whole thing yourselves." And so it became a self-perpetuating system. We just mixed in the yeast at the beginning and set the process in motion. With Septima Clark to provide the leadership, the program expanded into Georgia and other parts of the South.

Highlander's chief interest is in starting up programs. Sometimes we start off programs that get people going and our job is to get out of the way before we are run over. The Citizenship School project eventually became too big for us; in fact, it became bigger than all the rest of Highlander put together. When it gets to that stage, other people can take it over and operate it. Martin Luther King, Jr., whom I met when he was a junior at Morehouse College, asked if we would set up an educational program for the Southern Christian Leadership Conference (SCLC), and I asked him exactly what he wanted. After we talked about it several times, I said, "We've got a ready-made program that you can have. Take the Citizenship School program, it's too big for us." He backed off at first, but then he very meticulously went over the records and the costs and finally decided this was a program he wanted to recommend to his board. SCLC took that program over and we helped set it up. Septima Clark and Andrew Young (who had come to Highlander earlier in the year to work with the program) joined the SCLC staff.

In February of 1961, when we turned the Citizenship Schools program over to SCLC, I gave the following farewell talk to the prospective teachers who were in training at Highlander, the people who would be working on spreading the program throughout the South:

People learn faster and with more enjoyment when they are involved in a successful struggle for justice that has reached social movement proportions, one that is getting attention and support outside the movement, and it's socially big enough to go far beyond the individuals involved. It's a much bigger experience than anything you've had before as an individual. It's bigger than your organization, and it's qualitatively different, not just more of the same. I want the struggle for social and economic justice to get big and become so dynamic that the atmosphere in which you're working is so charged that sparks are darting around very fast, and they explode and create other sparks, and it's almost perpetual motion. Learning jumps from person to person with no visible explanation of how it happened.

To get something like this going in the first place you have to have a goal. That goal shouldn't be one that inhibits the people you're working with, but it should be beyond the goal you expect them to strive for. If your goal isn't way out there somewhere and isn't challenging and daring enough, then it is going to get in your way and it will also stand in the way of other people. Since my goal happened to be a goal of having a revolutionary change in this country and all over the world, it's unlikely to get in the way in the near future.

That was in 1961, a few months before the state of Tennessee revoked Highlander's charter and confiscated the school. Several years before, Bruce Bennett, the attorney general of Arkansas, instigated hearings to get at organizations in the South that were working for racial integration. He wanted the Tennessee State Legislature to investigate Highlander. The *Nashville Tennessean* wrote a scathing editorial denouncing the state of Tennessee for allowing itself to be a pawn of this guy, but that didn't stop the state from holding a hearing. When Bennett was showing the evidence he had about Highlander, he wrote "Horton" in the middle of a big blackboard and drew lines to people and groups that were against racism in the South: Anne Braden of the Southern Conference Educational Fund; Carl Braden, her husband, a lawyer; Charles Gomillion, the head of the civic association at Tuskegee Institute; Claude Williams; the Southern Conference for Human Welfare. He tried to show that all roads led to Horton. When they got through, the chairman asked me, "Will you deny that you're not the center of the Communist network in the South?"

None of the people or organizations were Communist, but they were all against racism. Then the chairman asked me, "What do you have to say about what the attorney general of Arkansas has just put on the board?"

"I don't have any comment," I said.

"Well, what do you think it proves?"

"It proves that you can write a name and write other names and draw lines between them."

Bruce Bennett (standing), attorney general of Arkansas, presents his analysis of Highlander's "subversive" influence before a Tennessee legislative investigating committee, 1959. *State Historical Society of Wisconsin.*

That was picked up by all the press, all the radio and television stations. I always tried to take advantage of situations like that.

Finally my lawyer told me, "Myles, you've got to quit making so much fun of these people. You're getting them so mad at you, they're going to put you in jail." But I used it. Entire high school and college classes came, because it was a show. My son, Thorsten, got out of grammar school to attend the hearing. A lot of the people in the press had been to Highlander and so they knew Thorsten. He was carrying a camera and wearing a big press badge they had given him so he could get in. At one point the chairman of the hearing said to me, "You don't seem to be concerned about yourself, but aren't you concerned about your children? They must be embarrassed and ashamed of having a person like you for a parent. What's going to happen to them?" Here was Thorsten not listening to a word he said, right up in his face taking his picture. The press played that up for all it was worth. To them he seemed to be getting along all right. That was really a show.

At the hearing they said that they were unable to substantiate the charge that Highlander was a Communist organization because every time evidence was produced, I denied it, but the Tennessee State Legislature nonetheless recommended that the district attorney find a way to close Highlander. Over a year later the district attorney decided they were ready to find a way to revoke our charter.

To get the thing started, he took a year to drill witnesses and call people to testify against Highlander. He found a woman who was very antagonistic toward the school. She picked some people out who had family members who had trouble with the law, and they were promised that if they testified against Highlander, they'd get out of jail. So they drilled these people, but they didn't do all their homework. They had one woman tell about passing by the library and seeing a black man and a white woman down on the floor naked. She said she remembered exactly when it was because she was pregnant with her son, Buddy, but he was born two years before the library was built. Later on, every one of them—including this woman—told me he or she had been paid. They wanted me to help them sue the prosecution for not having paid them more. Anyway, the district attorney took a year to get this thing set up.

To launch the case, the DA had to get some kind of start on it, so he arranged for Highlander to be raided while I was chairing an international residential adult education conference in Germany. It came out in court that they had purposely waited until I was away. County and state law officers, led by the DA, raided the school with Septima in charge and arrested her. Then they arrested Guy Carawan and two other men. The charges were that Highlander was selling beer without a license and running interracial classes. (Septima was serving Kool-Aid to high school–aged black kids from a Montgomery church group that was meeting at Highlander.)

That's the night the verse "We are not afraid" was added to "We Shall Overcome," and it was not only the beginning of that verse, but it started the trial that resulted in the state's confiscating Highlander's property.

Highlander didn't exist anymore, either physically or legally. Within two months of our leaving, all the buildings burned. We'd been there for about thirty years and never had a fire. We moved

Myles watching sheriff padlock Highlander's main building, 1959. *Highlander. Thorsten Horton.*

to Knoxville, where we knew it would be safer than out in the country, and settled into a big house in a black community, and we had a lot of support and protection from local labor unions. We had a lot of trouble, though: people tried to burn the buildings and firebomb us; they'd puncture tires and shoot out windows. But at least we survived there. We waited ten years and finally decided it would be safe to move out to another place in the country where Highlander is now located.

One of the things I had to do was take out a new charter for the school. I wanted to talk to the secretary of state, but I was told he was in Europe and wouldn't be back for another month. I told the people in his office that if I didn't have that charter in a week, I would sue the state of Tennessee. I had a tough reputation and in five days I had that damn charter just as I had written it. They've never bothered me since. I had to learn things like that. You have to find out how the system works. You can't function if you don't know.

We appealed the confiscation to the Tennessee Supreme Court, but they upheld the circuit court decision. After we appealed to the United States Supreme Court, Burke Marshall, head of the Civil Rights Division at the Department of Justice, told me to be prepared for a rejection of our Supreme Court appeal. He pointed out that when the Tennessee Supreme Court dropped the integration conviction to which we had proudly pleaded guilty (private school integration was illegal in Tennessee), we had lost our constitutional issue. He indicated that he believed this maneuver to prevent our appeal from reaching the U.S. Supreme Court was planned. Ignoring the integration issue needed in the lower court to convict Highlander and void our charter, the higher court upheld the conviction—selling beer without a license and operating Highlander for personal gain. We had been unaware that the repayment to someone who buys beer for the crowd required a license.

The Internal Revenue Service rechecked to see if I had gotten illegal money. After five years a letter arrived saying that their investigation had turned up overpayments on my part of $1,100. A lot of people wanted me to make a big issue of all this to show how Highlander had been a victim of Red-baiting, and to make us internationally famous, but I said, "Yeah, but we'll be out of business. I don't want to live on fame all my life, I want to work." So we just went ahead with the program.

We started right over again, getting a new charter under the name Highlander Research and Education Center that said we were going to do exactly the same thing we'd always done, and we started doing it. Losing our property was never the biggest issue. What was crucial was to get on with Highlander's work.

TEN

Charisma

Back during the heyday of the civil rights movement in Mississippi, I met an older black woman who told me, "We've got a Citizenship School down here." I asked her what that was and she told me, "Well, you know, I go out and teach people to read so they can vote. I can read a little myself. . . ." And I said, "That's great, where did you get the idea?" She told me, "I figured it out, and then I taught three other women to do it." She had no idea that anybody else was doing the same thing. She'd probably been to a conference where somebody was talking about Citizenship Schools and the idea was so simple, she could pick it up and make it her own.

It's only in a movement that an idea is often made simple enough and direct enough that it can spread rapidly. Then your leadership multiplies very rapidly, because there's something explosive going on. People see that other people not so different from themselves do things that they thought could never be done. They're emboldened and challenged by that to step into the water, and once they get in the water, it's as if they've never not been there.

People who work to create a decent world long for situations like this, but most of the time we are working with organizations. We cannot create movements, so if we want to be part of a movement when it comes, we have to get ourselves into a position—by working with organizations that deal with structural change—to be on the inside of that movement when it comes, instead of on the outside trying to get accepted.

When you're in an organizational period, which is most of the time, there can be many organizations without there being a movement. Organizations with nonstructural reform programs working to achieve limited goals can form alliances, but there's still no qualitative difference and no movement potential. During the civil rights movement, for instance, people came out of the labor movement, the black churches, the pacifist movement; people came who wanted social equality, and once the movement got under way, people who wanted to be where the excitement was were in it, people who wanted to get rid of their guilt were in it—it was so big that there was room for everybody.

A large social movement forces people to take a stand for or against it, so that there are no longer any neutrals. You've got to be on one side or the other. It's true that it forces some people to be worse than they would be, more violent than they would be, but it also forces some people to get behind the cause and work for it and even die for it. People have to understand that you can't make progress without pain, because you can't make progress without provoking violent opposition. If enough people want change and others stand in their way, they're going to force them out of the way. A revolution is just the last step of a social movement after it has taken a prerevolutionary form. Then it changes again —qualitatively—into something else. It's no longer a prerevolutionary movement, it's a revolution that transforms social, political and economic structures.

When you are part of a social movement, you discover that everything is so dynamic that nobody can make fixed plans and schedules anymore. During the civil rights movement you could schedule a demonstration around demands in, say, Birmingham, but you couldn't predict the dynamic situation that might develop. While Martin Luther King, Jr., was trying to figure out whether children should be allowed to demonstrate in Birmingham—in addition to his concern for the children, he was afraid that if they demonstrated and got killed or beaten up, there would be criticism of the movement—news came on the television that the kids had started demonstrating. So Martin announced that the children were going to be involved. This is what happens in a movement, and it's not anything that the best of planners and thinkers can control.

The job of Highlander was to multiply leadership for radical social change. The Citizenship School during the civil rights period is an example. It's been estimated that more than one hundred thousand people were reached by the Citizenship Schools. In my opinion, the truth is that nobody knows how many people were involved. They could have just said, "a helluva lot of people" and it would have been about as accurate. Social movements aren't subject to accurate record keeping. You can't reduce them to statistics.

In a social movement we are clearly part of a collective struggle that encourages us to increase our demands. One of the dynamic aspects of a social movement as opposed to an organization is that quite often in the latter, you'll bargain down to make concessions in order to survive. You have a limited goal, and you might say, "Well, we want to get ten street lights," and you'll get together and figure that you won't get ten, but you probably can get five. So you decide to tell them you want ten in order to get five. In a social movement, the demands escalate, because your success encourages and emboldens you to demand more. I became convinced that the seeds of the civil rights movement lay in the Montgomery bus boycott, because I'd seen the demands for fixed seating escalate to demands for blacks to be able to sit wherever they wanted. And then, when I saw the demands for blacks to be able to sit anywhere they wanted escalate into a demand for black drivers, I said, "This is the beginning of a social movement." The ante went up and finally escalated into demands that they do away with all public segregation. The boycott had started with the demand for fixed seating so that when the white section was filled, the whites couldn't come and take the blacks' seats in the back of the bus. As the blacks became emboldened by their action, they demanded and got total integration of the buses.

The success of something like the Montgomery bus boycott feeds a movement. It feeds the hopes of the people and gives them courage. It makes them daring and makes them demand more. The demands were within the confines of political democracy and social equality, however, and did not extend to economic structures, as I hoped they would. It wasn't because Martin Luther King, Jr., and other leaders didn't know the importance of economic demands, but because they felt that the traffic wouldn't bear it, that it would be too confusing and might divide the movement. Their fears may have been well-founded. When King made the speech at Riverside Church in New York in which he came out against the Vietnam War, SCLC and its board members and other civil rights leaders felt that including peace issues would divide and weaken the movement. For example, Bayard Rustin, a leading peace crusader, came down to the SCLC convention and made a long speech trying to persuade the delegates to keep the peace movement and the civil rights movement separate. The debate continued at the board meeting. Martin didn't say a word. He listened for a long time, and then he got up quietly and said, "I think we've been getting off the subject. The subject isn't 'What Martin Luther King's going to do,' the subject is 'What is the Southern Christian Leadership Conference going to do.' I took a position against the Vietnam War as a minister of the Gospel, and it isn't subject to debate. The subject is the Southern Christian Leadership Conference position, not mine." The board chairman just looked like he'd been hit with a sledgehammer. He stood there, stunned, because like everybody else he realized that what they were voting on was whether the SCLC should continue with or without King. As soon as that was clear, it didn't take them long to decide that they were going to incorporate opposition to the Vietnam War into their program. It was a powerful demonstration of King's integrity and his commitment to what he believed was right.

When I tried to get King to include economic democracy as a

Myles Horton, 1968, a moment of rest during the Poor People's Campaign, Resurrection City, Washington, D.C. *Mike Clark. Courtesy Guy and Candie Carawan.*

major demand, he didn't disagree that it was important, but he didn't think the time had come to make it a major issue.

Speaking at Highlander's twenty-fifth anniversary in 1957, less than two years after the movement got started, young Dr. King called on us to be "maladjusted"—to the evils of segregation, to the madness of militarism and to the tragic inequalities of an economic system that takes necessities from the many to give to the few.

Eight years later he was still advocating maladjustment to an unjust system. Speaking to a church group in 1964, he elaborated on the maladjustment theme and proposed a new world organization, "the International Association for the Advancement of Creative Maladjustment for men and women who will be maladjusted."

Later on he accepted the challenge to strike at the roots of the main source of violence—poverty itself. His campaign against world poverty would be the acid test of his belief in nonviolence. King envisioned combining the civil rights struggle for political rights and reforms of existing institutions with a revolutionary struggle to restructure the entire society.

At the time he was killed, he was meeting with the Memphis Sanitation Workers in their strike for dignity and a living wage. For months he had been making plans for a nationwide campaign against poverty. Economically deprived blacks, Native Americans, Hispanics and white Appalachian poor would march on Washington, D.C., and establish what would come to be called Resurrection City. Following a planning meeting for this Poor People's Campaign, I wrote Andrew Young:

I believe we caught a glimpse of the future at the March 14, 1968 meeting called by SCLC. We had there in Atlanta authentic spokesmen for poor Mexican-Americans, American Indians, blacks, and whites, the making of a bottom-up coalition . . . Martin, and those of you close to him, will have to spearhead the putting together of grassroots coalitions for the Washington demonstrations. This could lay the groundwork for something tremendously exciting and significant. Just as it is fitting for SCLC to make ending the war in Vietnam a basic part of the program, it would be fitting now, it seems to me, for SCLC to provide leadership for a bona fide coalition. No other organization has this opportunity and therefore, this responsibility.

King evidently judged that the time had come for a major societal change and that massive nonviolent, transforming action was called

Highlander's twenty-fifth anniversary, 1957. Martin Luther King, Jr., Pete Seeger, Charis Horton (Myles' and Zilphia's daughter), Rosa Parks, Ralph Abernathy. *Highlander.*

for. His experience and dedication to justice had radicalized him and given him new insights. His actions and his visions of uniting all the poor confused some of his followers, just as had his earlier opposition to war, but as always, he acted on his convictions "as a preacher, a man of God." He saw racial injustice as part of a larger problem and civil rights as part of a human rights struggle, including the right to life itself. Martin Luther King, Jr., was no longer saying that the poor can stop being poor if the rich are willing to become even richer at a slower rate. By 1966 he was saying, that for years

119

he had labored with the idea of reforming the existing institutions, a little change here, a little change there, but that now he felt quite differently. He had come to believe that it didn't do much good to be able to enter an integrated restaurant if you don't have the price of a hamburger.

While some of the goals of the civil rights movement were not realized, many were. But the civil rights movement as it was then cannot and should not be imitated. It was creative, and we must be creative. We must start where Martin Luther King, Jr., was stopped, and move on to a more holistic world conception of the struggle for freedom and justice.

The only problem I have with movements has to do with my reservations about charismatic leaders. There's something about having one that can keep democracy from working effectively. But we don't have movements without them. That's why I had no intellectual problem supporting King as a charismatic leader.

I experienced the temptations of becoming a charismatic leader in 1937, when I took a leave of absence from Highlander and became a labor organizer for the TWOC in McColl, South Carolina, and Lumberton, North Carolina. I made this change partly to see if I could do this kind of work and partly because I believed in the importance of getting people organized.

There was a long-drawn-out strike in Lumberton in which black people, Native Americans and white textile workers were out for two or three months. I was trying to keep the people's spirit up and give them something to do by having evening meetings in an outdoor lot near the mill, where we built a platform. In addition to getting some of the textile workers and their families who could make music to play and sing, I would have to do what they expected, which was to make a speech. There wasn't much else to occupy people while they were on strike. They didn't have any money to spend on entertainment. So we used to have at least a thousand people out every night, and I would get up and try to talk to them about the things I thought would be helpful. I talked about history, socialism, political action and cooperatives. I talked about events happening around the world. I had to think of something to talk about instead of just blasting out platitudes.

In the process of doing that, I learned how to hold the audience and how to keep them coming back every night. It got to be a game: I'd say to myself, "I'll see if I can talk about the Soviet Union

Billboard using photo from Highlander's twenty-fifth anniversary in 1957. *Highlander.*

tonight without scaring them," and I'd do it by talking about Moses leading the children out of bondage, and I'd cast around for other stories I could tell. In the process of doing that (with the help of the opposition, which always enhances your situation), the people got more and more enthusiastic, and I got carried away with this business of having so much power. I justified it by telling myself they might be learning a little something and were being exposed to some new ideas, but I found myself being impressed by having a following. One night I got to thinking about this and said to myself, "This is scary. This is the kind of thing I don't believe in, this is dangerous. Even if it's doing some good for the people, it certainly isn't doing me any good, and it's a temptation." That's when I thought about the Lord's Prayer, which doesn't say, "Save me from doing evil," it says, "Lead me not into temptation." It's the temptation you've got to watch, and there I was being tempted by the power that comes from charisma. My speaking certainly wasn't developing local leaders.

We had all kinds of trouble during that strike. First, the company tried to start a company union, and then they tried everything they could think of to frustrate us. We were stalling for time to get the labor board to act, and they were very slow, so we had to keep the spirit up. I'd never been in a situation where I had to do that kind of thing to a thousand people every night. I tried everything to keep them interested. The highway patrolmen were usually there, and I'd always thank them and the police for escorting me out of my hotel. I used to give them my hand, but they'd sit there, refusing to shake it, heads down. I used all this stuff as if I thought they were doing everything for me, and the strikers just loved it.

You don't just tell people something; you find a way to use situations to educate them so that they can learn to figure things out themselves. One time I pointed out the reporter for the local paper who was always standing around. He just filled his stories with lies every day. I told the strikers, "Now you listen very carefully to what I say; then tomorrow you read what he says and see if there's any difference." Then that night I'd ask, "What did you find out? What did he say?" I used all those things to educate people.

One day a fight broke out on the edge of the crowd and somebody called one of our strikers a bean eater. He shouldn't have gotten mad about it, because that's all he was eating—we didn't have any money for anything else. But the striker hit the heckler pretty hard and hurt him. A little scuffle broke out and it was stopped by our people. Neither one of them was arrested, but the next day I was indicted, charged with assault and battery, leading a mob and inciting a riot. I had been a block away on the platform. I was found guilty and sentenced to the chain gang. I appealed and in the meantime we settled the strike and got a contract. When I went back to court, the lawyer for the prosecution said they wanted to drop the case. "What do you mean, drop the case?" the judge asked him.

"You've got witnesses here, and the defendant has been convicted in a lower court and sentenced to the chain gang. What do you mean, drop the case?" The lawyer said, "Well, the strike's been settled in the meantime." He admitted right there in court that the only reason for the case was the strike. It had nothing to do with the truth. I made sure there were a lot of workers in court so they could begin to learn how the system worked.

It was in that same strike that they tried to run me out of town. One Sunday at about four o'clock in the morning there was a knock at my hotel door, and a young fellow who was a theological student at the University of the South in Sewanee—he had been to Highlander, but I hadn't known he was in Lumberton—came in and said, "Myles, I have to see you." When I asked him what he was doing in Lumberton, he said, "Well, I'm a summer pastor at the Episcopal church here and I just have to talk to you. Tomorrow at eleven-thirty all the ministers in the mainline churches are going to pray that you're removed from this town. I just couldn't sleep, I had to tell you. They're determined to get rid of you."

To make a long story short, the communication lines to God broke down somehow, and I was still there the next day, so the mill owners decided they'd better try something a little more immediate and they hired some people to kill me. It sounds dramatic, but if you know the labor movement at that time, you know people were killed. The killers came in the middle of the week to the busiest part of town during the busiest time of day, right across from the courthouse. One of the windows in my hotel room on the second floor looked out on the main street. All at once it was very quiet. I looked out the window and I couldn't see anything, couldn't see anybody. When I had gone out at noon to eat lunch, everything was just as busy as it always was. "Is this Sunday?" I asked myself. "This is the middle of the week, what's happening?" I went from window to window to see if I could figure out what was going on.

Then a car drove up under my window. I couldn't miss that car, because it was the only thing out there moving. There were four people inside, two in the front seat and two in the back. I just stood there and looked at them, and they looked up at me. Finally, one of them said, "We're coming to get you."

"Fine," I said.

They nudged each other, took a swig of beer—they were taunting me, so I knew they were the killers. This was it. The week before, a Holiness minister who was one of the union leaders came to my room and asked me if I had a pistol. I told him I didn't, and he said, "Well, you know there are all these threats about. You'd better keep this pistol." It was a great big one, and I just put it in the drawer. "It's loaded, six shots," he told me, and he left some more shells. I hadn't fired a pistol in years. My wife, Zilphia, was a good pistol shot—she could put a cigarette out—but when I shot one, I had to aim at the side of a building if I was going to hit anything. I could use a rifle, but I had never learned to shoot a pistol.

I went over and got that pistol and walked to the window with it in my hand, and those four men looked at me and looked at each other. One of them said, "What good is that going to do?"

"Well, I'd like to talk to you a minute," I said. "You know I like to organize."

"Yeah, but your organizing days are over."

"Well, the last thing I'd like to do is to try to help somebody get organized." They laughed, and I said, "You know you guys need to get organized."

"Why do we need to get organized?" one of them asked.

"Well, somebody's going to come in this door," I said. "You're going to get the key down at the desk." The hotel was owned by the company. "You're going to come up here and one guy's going to open that door and come in. And," I said, "I'm going to kill the first person that comes in. Next, another person is going to come in and I'll probably kill that person. When the third person comes in, it'll be a toss-up whether I kill him or he kills me. And the last person, he'll be able to kill me. There's no question about that. You've got to decide which ones of you I'll kill. I don't have a problem—I'm going to be killed—but you've got to decide which ones of you are going to be killed."

Of course you always know that such people think like a mob. They don't think individually. That's why the Klan is brave, that's why all mobs are brave. You've got to personalize it so they understand it's them. I asked one of the men in the front seat, "You have kids?"

"What's that to you?" he asked.

"Well, if you have," I said, "you don't want to die." I asked everyone if they had kids, and I held the pistol in my hand to emphasize the message, playing one against the other. I said, "Hey, you in the back seat. Are you going to be dead in a few minutes?

Or are you the one who's going to have to haul this guy in the front seat home? What are you going to tell his wife when you get there?" I just kept personalizing it, going round and round individualizing so that they'd think of themselves.

Then I told them, "That's why you need to get organized. You've got to vote on who's going to die. Are you people in the front seat going to die, or are you two in the back seat going to be the ones? Or one in the front, one in the back? Who's going to die?" I never asked, "Who's going to kill me?" I asked, "Who's going to die?"

They were sure they were going to kill me—that's why they were so brave—but they hadn't thought about themselves. In the meantime, I was standing there with this big old sheepleg (that's what we called those pistols), and I had the temptation to twirl it around as they do in the movies, but I was afraid I'd drop it. Finally they muttered to each other and just drove away.

Several years earlier when I was organizing the unemployed and the timber workers in Grundy County, I had had a related experience. I was driving through Altamont, the little county seat, and saw an old country store with three or four people sitting on the porch. When I passed by, they shouted at me, "Get out of town, you son of a bitch."

Well, I was going to have to come back down there and have some meetings, so I thought I'd better settle right there and not let it grow. I purposefully drove about a block beyond the store—I didn't slow down or anything—then I stopped, and backed up tortuously slowly. It took a long time, since I was just barely moving. As I inched my way there, I could see the men in the mirror. I didn't know what was going through their minds, but I wanted to get them worrying. I backed up and pulled up to the porch, but I didn't get close enough, so I backed up and pulled up again. I did two or three more maneuvers until I got as close as I could. Then I leaned out of the car and asked, "Did somebody speak to me?"

"No . . . no . . ."

"I thought I heard somebody. Hey you, did you speak to me?"

"No no no." They all denied it.

"Well, I must have been mistaken. Sorry to disturb you." I just drove on. That ended that—nobody ever hollered at me again in that town. Now, what did they think I could do? Three or four men sitting there, all of them as big as I was, what could I have done? Nothing. They could have come out and beat the hell out of me. They were thinking like a group. When I looked them in the eyes, they couldn't do it. I individualized the situation. That was what was behind the event in Lumberton.

I was still worried about my problems with charisma, but fortunately the strike in Lumberton was over. I told myself that it was time for me to get back into a situation where I wouldn't have any more of this temptation. I was very concerned about what it did to me, and I made myself a vow to continue as an educator instead of as an organizer.

That kind of experience and that kind of background made me very critical of people who were only charismatic leaders, but although Martin Luther King, Jr., was a charismatic leader, he wasn't just a charismatic leader; he was many other things.

King came out of a black church tradition where charismatic ministers are the norm. The ministers who have the big churches and are powerful influences in the black community are for the most part charismatic leaders, so this was a natural role for him. Because of his vision and because his vision involved hundreds of thousands of people, he didn't have the problem that somebody who only makes charismatic speeches or sermons has. He had many other roles and was tied into a reality that was much larger than a particular church. To characterize him solely as a charismatic speaker would be misleading and untrue.

Nevertheless, he was so impressive in this role that he cast a shadow over less able speakers and activists, who had the tendency to say, "Let Martin do it, Martin can do it so well, he can be the voice." And Martin accepted that role, although he might not have welcomed it.

I remember we used to have meetings and talk about strategy and discuss plans; somebody would come up with an idea, and Martin would ask different people what they thought. We'd arrive at some kind of consensus, and he would say, "Give me a couple of days to Martinize it and we'll do it."

Now what he really meant was to make the idea his own, so that when he spoke, it would carry with it all the power of his charisma. For some it was a privilege to contribute ideas that he might use, but those people who wanted to be leaders and have their names known felt overshadowed. Sometimes they got discouraged, because the tree was too big and too dense for undergrowth.

One of the criticisms I made to him was "You are so much the powerful leader that it's hard for people who work with you to have a role they can grow in. You could spend time making room under the tree and developing other leaders to take on some of the responsibilities."

Martin would say, "In my mind I know that has to be done, and it is happening," but from my perspective, it looked as if he had never developed anybody who could take his place after he was killed. Although there were a lot of people whose leadership was developed, they weren't widely known, and the lesser-known people who would have been the most competent to take over the Southern Christian Leadership Conference were not known well enough.

The best his replacements could do was try to create carbon copies of him, not become leaders in their own right. When it came to original thinking and being creative, people would say, "Well, what would Martin have done?" and try to do the same thing. To me, this was a great weakness in the movement. My point is that he never did get around to really doing what he knew was needed. I think that's a very difficult thing for a charismatic leader to do.

One thing I especially like about social movements is that even though they throw up charismatic leaders, most of the people who are part of them can learn to be educators and organizers. Highlander was able to play a role in developing educators because we were asked to do the educational work by both SCLC and the Student Nonviolent Coordinating Committee (SNCC). We trained the people who ran the Citizenship Schools and the voter registration drives, the noncharismatic people. That was when I learned, just as I had in the earlier industrial union period, that educational work during social movement periods provides the best opportunity for multiplying democratic leadership.

There is another important thing that social movements do: they radicalize people. That is, people learn from the movement to go beyond the movement. It may only affect a minority of the people, but there are so many people involved that thousands of them get radicalized. It might take a lifetime of nonmovement time to get that many people radicalized. So, if you had it within your power, you'd have one social movement after another.

When I say "radicalized," I'm talking about what happens to people who, through an experience of being part of a social move-

127

Desegregation workshop, coffee break, 1955. Charis Horton (center, front), Rosa Parks, students. *Highlander. Emil Willimetz.*

ment, understand that they must change the system. Now for years we had listened to pundits telling us we'd never do away with segregation, that people wouldn't change in our lifetime. But they did change.

What the pundits really meant was that you couldn't, through mere discussion, persuade people to have a change of heart and to give up their biases. I agree. But the civil rights movement started forcing people to change their actions. They were forced to change by mass demonstrations and boycotts and by blacks saying, "We're no longer going to take this, you're going to treat us like human beings, and we aren't going to wait through years of you changing your minds, changing your hearts, we're going to change them right now! We're going to march down that street, go in that restaurant, we're going to ride that bus. We're going to get action!"

People were forced to adjust their minds to what they had to do. And their hearts came poking along later. That's what a mass protest can do. It did change things, so the very people who said, "The South will never . . ." had to rationalize why they were willing to continue this way. And pretty soon, they said, "Well, we might as well get with it. The kids have to go to school, we can't keep on being racist, and talking about it around our kids." And so it moved people forward. Everybody profited. No question about it.

Any change from a place where you can be put in jail for being decent is a big change; a change from the fact that a black restaurant owner would be jailed or have his license taken away from him for serving a white, and a white restaurant owner would lose his for serving a black—now, that's progress, and it's measurable progress. That isn't to say it goes far enough, and that you don't have to fight constantly to keep those rights. Right now there are organized attempts to take them away. But it does say, for the time being, that we've made a step forward. There's been a structural change in the South's society that will never allow people to go back to where they were. The South will never again have a law saying that black people and white people can't eat together. Or go to school together. There will be all kinds of fudging and adjustments, but there has been a structural change that will be difficult to reverse.

The people who've been radicalized by their participation in a movement have taken that experience and asked, "What next? We didn't go far enough, we've got to have economic changes, we have to make further political changes, we have to change the structure of society, we have to have a different kind of system." If they only start down that road, then I say those people have been radicalized by being part of a social movement.

ELEVEN

Islands of Decency

I have a holistic view of the educative process. The universe is one: nature and mind and spirit and the heavens and time and the future all are part of the big ball of life. Instead of thinking that you put pieces together that will add up to a whole, I think you have to start with the premise that they're already together and you try to keep from destroying life by segmenting it, overorganizing it and dehumanizing it. You try to keep things together. The educative process must be organic, and not an assortment of unrelated methods and ideas. I try to get people away from saying, "Let's take

Highlander apart and see why it's been effective or when it's been effective." You can't do that. When you're a holist, that means you are a part of the whole; you not only hurt with someone who's hungry, you hurt with the prisoner who's suffering, you hurt with the whale that's suffering, you hurt with the people in South Africa, you hurt with everybody in pain.

Education is what happens to the other person, not what comes out of the mouth of the educator. You have to posit trust in the learner in spite of the fact that the people you're dealing with may not, on the surface, seem to merit that trust. If you believe in democracy, which I do, you have to believe that people have the capacity within themselves to develop the ability to govern themselves. You've got to believe in that potential, and to work as if it were true in the situation.

Because of this, you have to build a program that will deal with things as they are now and as they ought to be at the same time. They go together, the "is" and the "ought." Some people do all what "ought" to be, some do all what "is," but what you've got to do to be effective is do the "is" and the "ought" at the same time, or you won't be able to get practice and theory together.

I like to think that I have two eyes that I don't have to use the same way. When I do educational work with a group of people, I try to see with one eye where those people are as they perceive themselves to be. I do this by looking at body language, by imagination, by talking to them, by visiting them, by learning what they enjoy and what troubles them. I try to find out where they are, and if I can get hold of that with one eye, that's where I start. You have to start where people are, because their growth is going to be from there, not from some abstraction or where you are or someone else is.

Now my other eye is not such a problem, because I already have in mind a philosophy of where I'd like to see people moving. It's not a clear blueprint for the future but movement toward goals they don't conceive of at that time.

I know they're capable of perceiving and moving toward those humane goals because I've seen other people like them starting where they are. I know the potential is there. They don't know that it is there and that it is real, so I look at them with my other eye and say to myself, how do I start moving them from where they perceive themselves to be, to where I know they can be if

131

they work with other people and develop? I don't separate these two ways of looking. I don't say I'm going to look at where people are today, and where they can be tomorrow. I look at people with two eyes simultaneously all the time, and as they develop and grow, I still look at them that way, because I've got to remind myself constantly that they're not all they can be.

If you ever lose track of where people are in the process, then you have no relationship to them and there's nothing you can do. So if you have to make a choice between moving in the direction you want to move people, and working with them where they are, you always choose to work with them where they are. That's the only way you're ever going to be able to work with people and help them, because otherwise you separate yourself from them.

Then I set up a tension between where people are and where they can be, and I make people uncomfortable quite often because I keep pushing them, trying to help them grow. I make them unhappy and they say, "Myles, we just did this and we thought you'd let up, but the pressure is just the same as it was before." I tell them, "That's because you've just got to keep growing."

A few years ago I gave a speech at the Appalachian Studies Conference with Helen Lewis, a North Georgia woman who got radicalized in the civil rights period, became an anthropologist and sociologist, and is considered the mother of Appalachian studies. We talked about the way in which the economy of Appalachia was connected to the multinational corporations. I had taken a trip to Asia in 1986, and I presented an analysis of how Appalachia was a domestic Third World country in the sense that multinational corporations have exploited the Appalachian people, just as they have exploited the people in any Third World country. Somebody stood and said, "Myles, I've grown up knowing you and knowing Highlander, and about the time you got us to understand capitalism on a national level, you come along and tell us it's international. How are we ever going to figure it out?"

Stretching people's minds is part of educating, but always in terms of a democratic goal. That means you have to trust people's ability to develop their capacity for working collectively to solve their own problems.

Now at Highlander we had enough experience to know that people do have that capacity. In the early CIO days we saw people who had never heard of unions become good union members, take on fights, and develop and grow as people. In the civil rights movement we saw people come out of the fields and get in the voter registration line and be beaten up and shot at and become leaders and run for office and get elected. Since we've seen that, we don't think of ourselves as utopian.

My job is to try to provide opportunities for people to grow (not to make them grow, because no one can do that), to provide a climate which nurtures islands of decency, where people can learn in such a way that they continue to grow.

I grew up on a farm, so I know about growing things. And I still work in my garden. Gardening helps remind me how growing happens. Your job as a gardener or as an educator is to know that the potential is there and that it will unfold. Your job is to plant good seeds and nurture them until they get big enough to grow up, and not to smother them while they are growing. You shouldn't overwater them, overfertilize them or overwork them. And when bugs get on the plants, you've got to get rid of them so the plants can continue to grow.

People have a potential for growth; it's inside, it's in the seeds. This kind of potential cannot guarantee a particular outcome, but it's what you build on. What people need are experiences in democracy, in making democratic decisions that affect their lives and communities. The educational programs at Highlander have been called experiential-based education. Our interpretation during the first fifty years of Highlander's functioning was that the experience referred to was not the staff's but that of the people we were working with. This was the starting place. Their experience was sometimes enriched and extended by bringing to Highlander old-timers from the region—from the coalfields, the textile mills, the farming communities—to tell their stories, which we tried to capture by recordings or by taking notes to add to our archives of oral histories of the region. Another enrichment was the use of music and storytelling. The cultural aspects of Highlander have always played a very important role because we were trying to deal with the whole person and not just a segment of a person. In fact, the history of Highlander could in many important ways be told by the music— traditional songs and songs of struggle—that was brought there by the people.

What we tried to do could not be described as a method or a technique, but a process that had many strands One way I've pictured Highlander is as a long tapestry with a weft made up of many colors. During various periods, different colors would dominate over others. At times one color would be wide or become narrow or even fade out. Some colors, however, have always been present in the tapestry. New colors are continually added and old colors reappear. All of them are of a piece and blend in, and all are based on a love for humanity and trust in the ability of people to control their own lives eventually.

While Highlander always sought to be Highlander, not to imitate some other program, we knew that if we were to make a contribution toward transforming society, we'd have to be part of the larger world. We thought, however, that our contribution could be best made by doing it our own way.

If we are to have a democratic society, people must find or invent new channels through which decisions can be made. Given genuine decision-making powers, people will not only learn rapidly to make socially useful decisions, but they will also assume responsibility for carrying out decisions based on their collective judgment. The problem is not that people will make irresponsible or wrong decisions. It is, rather, to convince people who have been ignored or excluded in the past that their involvement will have meaning and that their ideas will be respected. The danger is not too much, but too little participation.

Popular education should give people experience in making decisions. Many take it for granted that people can make decisions, but actually, the majority of us are not allowed to make decisions about most of the things that are important. I have been put on the spot about the contradiction between my views on people making their own decisions and my action in making decisions that affect people's experience at Highlander, such as my insisting there can be no discrimination or lack of freedom of speech. I think, however, if you're going to help people make decisions, it's important to show them that the decisions they make must be responsible. Whenever you take a position, you've made a decision. The decision at Highlander from its beginning in the 1930s to practice social equality was a big one—with legal, practical and moral implications.

When people came to Highlander, we didn't just talk about their making decisions. We set up situations in which they actually had

Perry Horton, Jack Elliott, Lee Tom, Frank Hamilton, Guy Carawan, Highlander, 1953. *Courtesy Guy and Candie Carawan.*

to make them. In the 1930s and 1940s, when we were running workshops for labor union people, we would say to a group that came in, "Now, you have to learn to make decisions, to take responsibility, and the way to do it is not to listen to lectures, but to act. While you're here, you're going to have opportunities to make decisions and try your ideas out and act on them."

Of course this is very frustrating to people who have never had a chance to make decisions of importance in their lives, who think education is a counter with certain dishes labeled "arithmetic" and "history." Whenever you use the words "school" or "education," they think that's what they're coming for. They'd say, "Look, we came here to be taught. We were sent here by our unions to learn something, and you're supposed to tell us."

We would respond, "We know why you were sent here, and we are going to tell you, but we're going to tell you by giving you the opportunity of learning it yourself." And they would complain, "But we don't know what to do." And then I would say, "Of course you don't know what to do, you've never had a chance to do this before, and all you know about school or workshops is what you've had when you were growing up. This is something else. I understand your problem, but this is the way it's going to be. We're not, however, going to plunge right into it. Last week when we had people here like you, we asked them, from their experience, to recommend a program for you. Now, here is that program. My suggestion is that you follow their recommendation for one day. Before you leave, you will be asked to recommend a program for the next group."

Once, I thought that somebody who had been doing some expert research and action work on the West Coast would be appropriate for one of the workshops we had at Highlander. He'd always wanted to attend, and I'd told him that this time he could—we didn't have observers, but he could come and make a contribution. He could be a part of the group on the basis of his experience, which they could consider as an alternative form of action. But, it turned out that the workshop went a different direction entirely and didn't deal with what I thought it might. Apparently, what he knew wasn't appropriate to the concerns of the students. He kept asking when he was going to speak, and finally I had to tell him, "Look, I made a mistake. I told you that we'd be talking about certain things, but it didn't turn out that way. We can't get outside the experience of these people, we can't get beyond the things that tie into their experience or we'll break that connection and the whole process will be rejected. It's not like an exam, where you regurgitate and get credit for it."

"You mean you brought me all the way here . . . ?"

"That's exactly what's happened." And he never did speak.

If you want to have the students control the whole process, as far as you can get them to control it, then you can never, at any point, take it out of their hands. People know the basic answers to their problems, but they need to go further than that, and you can, by asking questions and getting them stimulated, coax them to move, in discussion, beyond their experience and start saying things like "Well, I heard old Joe over the mountain talking, and . . ." and "Myles, you were telling us one time when you were up visiting us about something . . . what was that you were talking about?" And when you begin to expand the experience and share your own, people will ask each other questions.

Boundaries get pushed further and further so that it's appropriate for me, in a workshop, at a given stage in the discussion, to provide an illustration of something that I saw in South Africa, or in Asia, or in Alaska among similar kinds of people in similar situations. The examples would be within people's experience and not break the continuity of the workshop. They would be new, in some ways, but would be part of the whole process.

If you listen to people and work from what they tell you, within a few days their ideas get bigger and bigger. They go back in time, ahead in their imagination. You just continue to build on people's own experience; it is the basis for their learning.

When you provide people with opportunities to learn for themselves by making decisions, there are two concepts that are central: social equality and freedom of speech. They both involve the understanding and protecting of minority rights. These concepts are not abstractions for the people I've worked with. Whoever was running a Highlander workshop would talk about the dangers of making decisions that excluded some people and made the process undemocratic. They'd also point out that exclusion means that the group would lose the benefit of people who have minority ideas that sometimes become majority ideas later on. It's important to stress that at a workshop you can't make decisions that would prevent any ideas from coming to the surface. All objections have to be heard, all disagreements allowed to come out into the open. You have to make decisions that everybody can live with. The decisions have to be on that level—universal.

The role of the workshop leader is to help people see that they can make any decision they want to, so long as it applies to everybody. The reason they can't make decisions that don't apply to everybody is that they might be the "everybody" it didn't apply to.

Ideas are tools: you can play with them, turn them around, look at them, use and test them, and if students do this at Highlander, they can go back and duplicate the process, because they understand it. If they don't understand the process, they may be able to go back and mouth it, but they can't live it.

Practice in making small decisions can also add to people's experience and connect them to larger issues. For example, it is important to learn to make decisions about what you buy, because it could affect your health. It could have to do with your social philosophy and how you make decisions about buying something that

137

was made by slave labor, or from a company like J. P. Stevens that was resisting unionization, or from South Africa. Any decision that has social ramifications, however segmental and small, can be an important decision in which value judgments play a role. What we need to do as educators is to make people aware of the fact that those decisions are important and that they should know how to get the information necessary to make those decisions. What is essential is that people get the practice of making decisions and that they come to know they should consciously make them at every point. I realize that most of us can't make decisions about big things in society, but educators should try to help people make conscious decisions at every point: long- and short-range decisions, small decisions, decisions that affect only a few people and those that affect many. All of them are important.

However, I wouldn't want a society where everybody has to make the same decision. That would be terrible, because these lowest common denominator decisions would avoid dealing with social issues. I can't imagine a world in which there isn't conflict growing out of different decisions, and I think we have to set up the procedures that take into consideration minority decisions and decisions that seem completely crazy, yet have a place in our thinking, since they may grow into noncrazy decisions. History tells us that the minority decisions have become the majority decisions, and that any society which doesn't allow for this to happen is going to die.

We were not a therapy organization, and we were not a vocational training place. We were a group of educators helping people learn how to be social activists. The people we selected had already shown some promise as potential leaders who would have some responsibility when they went back home.

The history of Highlander is the history of the struggles in the South over the last fifty-five years, but Highlander also has a history of its own. We avoided implementing programs that other less cutting-edge organizations or institutions were doing. We tried to find ways of working that did not duplicate what was already being done. To be true to our vision, it was necessary to stay small and not get involved in mass education or in activities that required large amounts of money (which would make it tempting to do the kinds of programs that money was available for). We found that as

Workshop in Mississippi, 1964. Aimee Horton, Lawrence Guyot, Dickie Flowers, Myles Horton. *Highlander. Thorsten Horton.*

our programs grew during the labor movement period and the civil rights period, the activities required more funds and more staff members. We solved the problem of staying small by spinning off programs that were already established and were willingly taken over by organizations less interested in creating new programs. The CIO took over our program for training directors of labor education and much of the stewardship training, as well as other Highlander labor activities. In the civil rights period, we spun off the Citizenship School program—probably one of Highlander's most significant activities—to SCLC. These spin-offs enabled Highlander to concentrate on cutting-edge programs that no one else in the region was undertaking.

I do not believe in neutrality. Neutrality is just another word for accepting the status quo as universal law. You either choose to go along with the way things are, or you reject the status quo. Then you're forced to think through what you believe. If you're going to be for something, then you have to know there's an opposite that you're against. That runs contrary to the traditional thinking

139

in this country: you're supposed to be positive, for something but not against something. But it's impossible to be for anything without being against something. You have to clarify what you're against, and once that's figured out, you have to determine how to do something about it. You say, "OK, this is the kind of world I'd like to see, these are the kinds of values that seem important to me." Then you have to figure out how to work so that it affects people. What you do with all these ideas and concepts and hunches is a matter of experience and then a testing. You have a hypothesis and you test it out. You find that some of it is good and some of it is bad. Then you revise it and you have another hypothesis that you can test out.

When we first started Highlander, we had ideas that we tried to apply to a situation. We started by moving from theory to practice. It took us only a few months to learn that we were starting the wrong way, because we weren't reaching the people. We realized it was necessary to learn how to learn from these people, so we started with the practical, with the things that were, and we moved from there to test our theories and our ways of thinking. We reversed the usual process; instead of coming from the top down and going from the theoretical to the practical, trying to force the theory on the practical, we learned you had to take what people perceive their problems to be, not what we perceive their problems to be. We had to learn how to find out about the people, and then take that and put it into a program. Sometimes that knowledge ties into some theories, but if the theories don't fit the practice, then you say the theory is wrong, not the other way around. Before, we had been saying that if the practice didn't fit the theory, the people were wrong, and we tried to force the people into the theory. It's the way we are all socialized by education.

We had accepted a theory we had grown up with in school: that the way we'd been taught was the right way to teach. But we were now in an out-of-schooling situation where the ways of learning were different. The problem was we didn't know that. We tried to impose our school experience on this different situation. We didn't understand that the socialization we went through made us willing to be bored to death for years while we accumulated all kinds of useless knowledge. We had to pass exams because we had to finish high school, go to college, do graduate work. We found that all these things that made us learn didn't connect with the people we were dealing with, the out-of-school people. So we had to unlearn and relearn from them. It was only then that we could begin to build a base for Highlander that gave us roots among the people and in their problems.

One of the problems for me, and I guess for all the staff members, was that we were used to learning from our reading, and a lot of the people we were dealing with couldn't write and couldn't express themselves very well verbally, so we had to arrive at other ways of finding things out, other ways of communicating. We were forced to learn by watching people. I remember one very intelligent man who would grunt instead of talk. Once we learned to interpret his grunts we got pretty good at knowing when he was for or against something.

There are problems when theory takes over from practice. A friend of mine, the poet John Beecher, invited me to speak at the college in California where he was teaching. It was to have been a small meeting with a handful of people, but the John Birch Society put out posters and went on a TV program exposing me as a dangerous Red in order to warn people against me. The result was that, with the John Birch Society as my press agent, I had a packed house.

When I got there, the Birchers were at the door handing out leaflets. I was introduced by a theological student from the University of the South at Sewanee who had been to Highlander. He talked about what I believed in and about Highlander. It was kind of flattering, so I got up and said, "I was fortunate to have two introductions: one from my friend here who has been at Highlander, and one from the Birch Society, which gave these leaflets outside." I thought it was a good idea to have introductions from two different points of view, so I said, "My position is that Highlander is halfway between what our friends say and what our enemies say. It gives a more accurate description, because they both overdo it."

My speech concerned the use of nonviolence to bring about change in the South. I had a good responsive audience. During the question and answer period, somebody got up—he was with a group of people with banners, one of the sectarian Communist groups—and said, "You're misleading the people, coming here and telling us that the strategy in the South has to be nonviolent protest. And you're betraying the black people by saying that nonviolence is the way to deal with this problem." I believed very firmly that the only way you could deal with the problem of civil rights was through nonviolence. I said, "I'm not a pacifist, but I think that there are times when nonviolent protest is the appropriate thing, and I think this situation is one of them, so I approve of it and I'm willing to explain it."

According to this group, I was selling the people out, advising them wrongly. For them the only solution to the problem was armed action. They said blacks had to be armed, and they had to tell people they had to be armed, and they had to fight for it and so on. And I said, "I appreciate that contribution to the discussion, and I'd like to make it clear that I think it's a legitimate theory. It's an opinion of what's the right strategy, and I don't rule it out as something to discuss, I just happen to disagree with it. But," I said, "My position is, if you believe in something, then you act on it. Now, I say I believe in nonviolent protest, so I go on demonstrations. I'm willing to put myself on the line. I get beaten up, I get put in jail. I believe in racial equality and I want to demonstrate my belief by my actions. Since you're Marxists, you must believe in theory and practice, and I'm sure you agree with me that if you believe in something, you should act on it. When I get back to the South, I will arrange for you to be invited into Mississippi, where the struggle is now, and you can come down and demonstrate what it is you believe. You'll have a chance to present, in the most effective way, your argument. Give me your names so I can get in touch with you. Bring your guns and demonstrate to the black people the validity of your position."

I didn't get any responses, so I said, "Could it be that you want black people to test out your ideas? And get killed, and find out whether it works or not? You wouldn't be doing that, would you?"

They got up and walked out as a body. They didn't want to talk about it, but the answer was obvious: they wanted black people to test out their theories. I knew this answer all along. I just set it up so I could educate people about practice and theory.

When people open something up to you, you've got to deal with it. You have to act on what you believe, and when people see how you act, they understand what you believe. Since we learn to do by doing, we learn to make decisions by making decisions. If I was

142

going to help people make decisions, I couldn't give them a speech on the importance of decision making, but I could demonstrate, by my making decisions, that this was something they could and should do.

TWELVE

Workshops

Learning at Highlander revolved around our residential workshops, although they were only one part of the whole process we engaged in to contribute to social change. The people who were sent to the workshops by their organizations were not sent as individuals. They all had experience working in their own communities, in unions or in other organizations. They also had a potential for grassroots leadership.

Grassroots leaders are not official leaders but people who are recognized as having leadership qualities by the people they live and work with. To put it in union terminology, they are shop stewards, people close to the rank and file who are looked to for advice and leadership. In a community organization, where the structure is not the same as in unions, they are the people that others look to for advice and encouragement. For example, in the South before the civil rights movement, there were many black beauticians and barbers who had the potential for grassroots leadership. They provided services for black people that whites refused to, and because their incomes were independent of the white establishment, they couldn't be threatened economically. That's why we turned to them when we began the Citizenship Schools program. They were also involved in the desegregation of buses, schools and colleges.

Announcing a workshop on

NEW LEADERSHIP RESPONSIBILITIES

Highlander Folk School
Monteagle, Tennessee

January 15–17, 1961

Purpose: To explore the opportunities offered in the Beautician's profession, for promoting justice and equality in the South.
Background: The new democratic initiative taken by Negroes in the South is characterized by direct, specific and immediate public social action.

The requirements now are for a new kind of leadership which is voluntary, and which can speak out openly, hold office in community organizations for integration, and publicly promote the cause.

The Beautician's profession enjoys complete freedom, and has also some unusual opportunities for direct action within its scope of contacts and influence. Someone has said "The Beauty Salon is a center of communication and influence."

Furthermore, the profession may be considered to represent a new opportunity for leadership of professional women in social action.
Participants: Members of the Beauticians' profession *only.*

The reason we chose to work on grassroots leadership was that when you're trying to break out of the conventional way of doing things, that is, a top-down authoritarian way, you have more chance

145

of influencing someone who hasn't been molded into the hierarchical system, and hasn't already been socialized to operate from the top. People who are just beginning to understand themselves as leaders are also more open. Probably even more important, they can be held responsible by the membership, not just by the top officials of the organizations that sent them to Highlander. Whatever strength and influence they have will be based on their serving the people who have accepted some of their leadership. They are also accessible to their people on an everyday level, whereas with institutional leadership, you have to make an appointment.

The people we wanted to come to Highlander were those who are free to act, who are not constrained by institutional roles except for their perception of the situation and their relationship to others. They keep the people behind them, and to do this they have to act democratically.

This freedom to act, to take risks, implies freedom to learn and to accept the idea that you can build your strength from the bottom up instead of the top down. These individuals build their strength on representing the people instead of the officialdom of some organization.

One of the lessons I've learned about bureaucracies is that although they are not made up of evil people, they can do something bad to good people. These same people I'm talking about, these grassroots leaders, sometimes went back to their unions and became presidents, organizers, even international presidents of international unions, but then they got to the place where they were no longer grassroots; they moved into bureaucratic situations where they became more responsible to the top than to the stream of people at the bottom, the people that gave them power in the first place. They felt that their power came from being part of the national and international teams. In many cases they became what you might call humane bureaucrats. They weren't bad people at all—they still talked the same way—but they acted differently. Watching this in the 1930s and 1940s, I came to the conclusion that the bureaucratic system is an inevitable disease that afflicts all organizations and governments. Often it is spread by good people who are made to do bad things—or less than good things—because of their separation from the people who were the original source of their power.

Highlander in its first fifty years advocated working from the bottom up, and encouraged putting decision making in the hands of working people. However, many people who came to Highlander didn't value their own experience because they were never allowed to or taught how. They had been taught to listen to somebody else and to follow directions, though they had come with an enormous amount of experience. They just hadn't learned from it and therefore didn't value this experience. You can have a perception of people's problems, but you have to use your judgment about the level of understanding people have of the problem they've come to deal with.

The men and women who came to the workshops had the potential for multiplying what they learned and for dealing with structural changes—not little reforms but real, basic changes in the structures of their communities. Highlander worked with people who were dealing with important issues. Anything that one person can do alone is not worth doing when you're dealing with social problems. If a problem is that small, then the goal is too limited. There is a popular theory that if you give people simple enough goals that they can reach without too much effort, they will get a sense of success, and that success will build them up. I think that's a lot of malarkey. If a goal isn't something very difficult, all that people will learn to do is to tackle little problems. You can't develop any valuable leadership if you don't teach people that they can deal with big problems.

At Highlander we wanted people to deal with how to change society, not with smaller issues such as trying to get a street light or a road crossing sign installed. Those issues are important, but they are not ways to transform society. We only invited people who we perceived were dealing with basic changes in the structure of society.

When I was on staff at Highlander, there were times when we had to say to some people, "You can't come because the problem you want to deal with isn't big enough." On the other hand, sometimes we found groups of people who were not very successful in their efforts, but in our opinion they were dealing with structural changes in society, problems that didn't lend themselves to easy solutions. If they could break through and learn how to deal with their problems, they would have something that could be multiplied and might lead to structural changes in society just as the Citizenship Schools did.

The people who came to Highlander had problems that we had

no answers for. Nobody did. We weren't experts; we just tried to help people work out solutions. Highlander students were experiencing problems they couldn't cope with; social problems, group problems, problems of consequence that are hard to deal with. For instance, some people have had to deal with the problems created by strip mining in their own communities, but since strip mining occurs all over the United States, and in Asia and Europe, it's obviously not just a local problem. As educators, we had to learn about the size of the problem, and at the same time we had to know the situation of people who wanted to come.

There were no given answers to the problems we dealt with, and we don't pretend to have any. They have to be worked out in the process of struggling with the problem. The knowledge needed for the solution has to be created. The Highlander workshop is part of a continuum of identifying a problem and finding other people who are trying to deal with it. The people who come to the workshops have a lot of knowledge that they don't know they have. Highlander gives them a *chance* to explore what they know and what some people we bring in as resources can share with them. Then they have to go back home and test what they learn in action. If they have learned anything useful they can teach others because it is now part of their knowledge, not something merely handed to them. Highlander has been a stop in the continuum of defining and trying to solve an important problem, a place to think and plan and share knowledge.

Highlander workshops are based on the mining of the experience that the students bring with them, their awareness that they have a problem to deal with, and the relationship of that problem to conflict. They have to be opposed by mine owners or government, prevented from eating in some restaurants or denied their fair share of public resources. They must know that they have problems which can't be solved on a personal level, that their problems are social, collective ones which take an organized group to work on. For this reason, an individual can't come to a Highlander workshop with a personal problem. People have to be selected by their organizations and report back to the organizations that sent them.

For example, Rosa Parks came to a Highlander workshop shortly before she refused to move so that a white man could have her seat on the bus. She was sent to the workshop by E. D. Nixon, Alabama NAACP president and vice president of the Brotherhood of Sleep-

Participants in desegregation workshop listen to tape recording, summer 1955. Rosa Parks at far end of table. To her right, hands clasped, Dr. F. D. Patterson, director of the Phelps-Stokes Fund; to his right, C. H. Parrish; Septima Clark. *Highlander. Emil Willimetz.*

ing Car Porters, and by Virginia Durr, a white woman from Montgomery, Alabama, who had been fighting racial segregation for years. Rosa Parks had been the executive secretary of the NAACP in Montgomery for a number of years and was well known in the community. At the end of our workshops we reviewed and critiqued the sessions and then asked the participants what they were going to do when they got home. Rosa Parks said that she didn't know what she could do in "the cradle of the Confederacy," but at a later workshop she described her first workshop experience:

At Highlander, I found out for the first time in my adult life that this could be a unified society, that there was such a thing as people of different

149

races and backgrounds meeting together in workshops, and living together in peace and harmony. It was a place I was very reluctant to leave. I gained there the strength to persevere in my work for freedom, not just for blacks, but for all oppressed people.

When she returned to Montgomery and refused to move to the back of the bus, even though her action was not prearranged and she acted individually, Rosa Parks operated with the full knowledge that for at least two years black people in Montgomery had been trying to set up a test case on the segregated buses. She knew the consequences of her action; she knew she would be arrested. But she didn't think she was breaking the law, because she didn't think the segregation law, which was unjust, should be there. With that knowledge, Rosa wasn't only acting as an individual, she was acting in a way that was consistent with the beliefs of the black organizations in Montgomery, just as she was sent to a Highlander workshop by some of the same organizations. But Highlander was only one of many learning experiences in the lifelong preparation for Rosa Parks' unique form of protest, which launched the civil rights movement. By refusing to move from her seat, this gentle woman set thousands marching and made it possible for the rest of us to stand tall.

I think of an educational workshop as a circle of learners. "Circle" is not an accidental term, for there is no head of the table at Highlander workshops; everybody sits around in a circle. The job of the staff members is to create a relaxed atmosphere in which the participants feel free to share their experiences. Then they are encouraged to analyze, learn from and build on these experiences. Like other participants in the workshops, staff members are expected to share experiences that relate to the discussions, and sources of information and alternative suggestions. They have to provide more information than they will be able to work into the thinking process of the group, and often they must discard prepared suggestions that become inappropriate to the turn a workshop has taken. Consultants who were brought to Highlander at considerable expense were sometimes not allowed to make presentations, because what they had to offer did not provide answers to the problems raised by the participants. Often we had to send back movies and pamphlets without using them. Each session had to take its own form and develop according to the students' needs.

One time, the CIO sent their new educational director, Kermit

Eby, to Highlander three days into a workshop. He had been a Brethren minister and a missionary in China, and later he became a Hegelian Marxian, a religious radical, but he had no experience with factory workers. The CIO told him to go down to Highlander and work with me for a week because they thought it would be beneficial for him. The night he arrived, I told him, "Get to know the people, there'll be some good discussions you can take part in."

He said, "No, I'll make a speech," because he was used to preaching and lecturing.

I told him, "I don't know, Kermit, the students aren't geared to that kind of thing. I'd just as soon you don't make a speech. Go ahead if you want to, but the students have the right to tell you not to make that speech, or not to make another speech, and the right to butt into the middle of your talk and say what they think. I can't stop them. That's how we operate this place."

He said, "I think that's a mistake," and I said it might be, but that's how it was.

The next day Kermit got up and gave a very learned lecture that graduate students would have had a hard time understanding unless they were Hegelian scholars. The students were so fascinated with it that they sat there and listened to all the big words they didn't understand, punching each other whenever he talked about the thesis, the antithesis, the synthesis and other Hegelian ideas. Every time certain terms came up, they'd say, "Thesis it! Thesis that!", playing on his words. When the students wandered off—either physically or mentally—Kermit became terribly upset.

"They didn't pay attention," he said to me.

I had to tell him, "Kermit, in most schools you have a captive audience, and the students are going to listen to anything because they have to take an exam on it. They have a motivation to listen to anything you say. The people here at Highlander don't get grades. When they go home, they're going to get the hell beat out of them for doing some of the things they're going to do, so they have to get something they think they can use. They don't see how what you said ties into where they are. But don't worry too much about it, being here is a good way for you to learn this kind of thing."

His answer to that was "I'm not here to learn, I'm here to teach."

Later that day the students came to me and said, "Get rid of that guy."

All I could say was "But he's the national education director."

"We don't care," they said. "If he wants to help us, fine, but we don't have time to listen to his speeches."

I went to Kermit and told him what the students had told me, as gently as possible. He replied that he wasn't going to talk down to people. "They don't want you to talk down to them," I said. "They want you to talk *to* them, *with* them. You're not communicating."

He couldn't understand that, so I told him, "The students have the authority at Highlander, and they'll exercise it to decide what to do about you. You'll have to let me help you, or you'll have to leave."

He said he wouldn't leave. "You will too," I said, "they're big guys. They close down plants; they don't fool around. They could just pick you up and carry you off. You just listen to me and learn about what happens here or you're going to have to learn the hard way."

I just scared the hell out of him, but he stayed anyway. Before leaving, he got up and apologized to the students. Later he became one of our most ardent champions. Sometimes people who didn't understand what we did at Highlander had to learn that decision making was at the center of our students' experiences.

The best teachers of poor and working people are the people themselves. They are the experts on their own experiences and problems. The students who came to Highlander brought their own ways of thinking and doing. We tried to stimulate their thinking and expose them to consultants, books and ideas, but it was more important for them to learn how to learn from each other. Then they could go back to their communities and keep on learning from each other and from their actions. Since our workshops were brief—a couple of weeks or even a long weekend—they had to be tied to learning that had already taken place and was related to a problem they were still working on. We served as a catalytic agent to hasten the learning process.

It goes without saying that in our concept of education, there were no grades and no examinations. We also claimed no neutrality in presenting facts and ideas. What we sought was to set people's thinking apparatus in motion, while at the same time trying to teach and practice brotherhood and democracy.

• • • •

We have always made a number of assumptions about workshops. First, a workshop has to have a goal arising out of a social problem that the students perceive; second, people have within themselves the potential, intelligence, courage and ability to solve their own problems; third, the Highlander experience can add to and enrich the educational experience that the students normally would have; fourth, in addition to learning from their peers during the workshop experience, the Highlander staff members should have an opportunity to interact in the field with the students.

The most important parts of a workshop come from what has happened in a community before the workshop itself, and what happens when people go home and act. Highlander never existed solely as a workshop organization. We always worked with communities, and this field program and the residential program fed each other. Recruiting for workshops is a circular process, because once you are established as being useful, people who have valued the workshop experience always want to introduce others to it.

A fifth aspect of Highlander workshops is that the factual information and analysis presented has to be tailored to the expressed needs of the participants. It is meant to be usable knowledge that can help when people return home. In order to facilitate this, the composition of the Highlander staff has to be reevaluated according to the needs of each major period or program it is involved in. We had to find appropriate staff members for the CIO, civil rights, Appalachian and now the international phases of its existence. The questions have always been: who will be of most use, and how can we minimize the differences between the staff members and the people we work with so that the former can function in the dual roles of workshop leader and participant in the circle of learning.

Finally, follow-up always deserves special attention, because sometimes students develop programs on their own that require assistance, financial aid and, sometimes, legal defense. Because Highlander only gets involved in these programs on request, it is also important to find ways to keep in touch with the students and their communities.

In the workshop itself, insofar as the leader has solidarity with the people in that circle of learning, the people understand that their problems are taken seriously. Care must be exercised that the circle is not broken. If someone says, "I'm personally upset because my organization won't do something," the workshop leader would try to shift the focus of the complaint from personal upset to the functioning of the organization, by saying, "Let's talk about what the organization isn't doing that you're upset about."

If someone else said, "I have problems with my family," we'd say, "Well, that's not what we're here to talk about in the workshop—not that the problem is unimportant—but this workshop is about dealing with segregation. Maybe later on after class we could get together and talk about that problem if you want to, but in the workshop we have to talk about things that concern everybody in the group."

The same things hold for people in the workshops if they want to give a communistic speech, a born-again Christian speech or a KKK speech. We'd say, "This is not part of the problem, not what we're talking about. There's a room available after the workshop where you can meet with people if they want to come and hear your speech. It's not what we're doing here."

In our workshops people can talk about anything that is appropriate to the problem they come with. The limits of discussion have nothing to do with freedom of speech, but with keeping to the topic we agreed on beforehand. Within that topic you can talk from any point of view. A person can say, "As a Catholic I don't like this," or "As a Communist I don't like this," or "As a Klansman I don't like this," but you can't come and make a partisan speech. All of the participants, equally, can discuss what everybody else is discussing. There can be no discrimination within the topic, and it is the role of the workshop leader to keep the group to its subject.

Sometimes there were troubles. People would say to me, "You believe in freedom of speech. Will you let me come into the workshop and speak?" And I'd say, "You mean can you come in and take over this workshop when people have come here to talk about a specific problem? What you're insisting on would deny them *their* freedom of speech."

I recall a religious fundamentalist preacher who probably thought we were Communists, and he needed to come out and save us by warning the students against communism. He asked if he could give a speech.

Another time, a fine young man who had been working with Highlander joined one of the sectarian Communist groups, in this case a Maoist organization, and he had just seen the new day and had all the answers. He came out and said, "I have great news and I'd like to talk to people here about what's happening."

I asked him what had happened and he said, "Chairman Mao has just endorsed our party in the United States, and that means we can be the vanguard of the movement."

Then he asked me, "Aren't you impressed?"

"For an American radical party I would be much more impressed if a couple of factory workers endorsed your party," I said. "As far as speaking at Highlander, we have a workshop going and the people came here for that. It wouldn't be fair for them to talk about what only you're interested in. We're trying to build a program on what they're interested in."

Freedom of speech is essential, but license to keep other people from speaking is not freedom of speech. Highlander workshops have been guided by two principles: nobody can be discriminated against, for any reason, and there is freedom to say anything or take any position on the topic of the workshop. These conditions are understood beforehand by the participants. However, sometimes a person comes up with something that is not only off the topic, but is meant to provoke everybody else, get everybody upset and change the topic to his or her agenda. One particular case involved Charles Hayes, now a congressman from Illinois but then an official with the Packinghouse Workers. This union had a very good nondiscrimination policy, and a lot of white people had difficulty adjusting to it. Even when they did adjust, they couldn't bring themselves to say the word "Negro," which was used before people started saying "black." They were used to saying "nigger."

At the workshop there was a tall white Texan. He was a nice guy and trying hard to fit in. He didn't have intellectual problems about antiracism, but he had cultural and social habits, and one of them was that he couldn't say the word "Negro" right. He didn't say "nigger" because he knew that wasn't allowed in our workshops, so he'd say "Neg-ro" or "Ni-gro," struggling to pronounce "Negro." The way he said it was riling up some of the people in the workshop and making it hard to get on with the issues we wanted to talk about.

Charlie Hayes, who could be somewhat intimidating, finally said to him, "Look, I've been trying to tell you to say 'Negro.' Now since we're here at Highlander, I'm going to pay my respect to

Zilphia Horton leading strikers in song, 1940s. *Highlander*.

education and I hope you can learn through Myles' way how to say 'Negro,' but if you can't, I've got another way to teach you."

Obviously Charlie's method was going to be rather direct, so he added, "Maybe I can help you learn Highlander's way. You told me you grew up on a farm and you grew cotton."

The Texan asked Charlie why he brought that up, and Charlie said, "Well, you can say 'grow,' can't you? Say 'grow!'"

So the Texan said "grow" and Charlie said "good," and then he put his hand on the Texan's knee and asked him, "What's this?" The Texan answered that it was his knee. Charlie continued: "You don't have any trouble saying 'knee' and saying 'grow.' Now just say 'kneegrow.' That's Highlander's way of teaching. I hope that's enough, because my way is a little rougher."

There are different ways of dealing with problems. Charlie Hayes said, "There are two ways of doing it, Highlander's way or my way," but you can't let instances of discrimination pass. You have to do something right then.

156

Pete Seeger and friends: (left to right) Sarah Ogan Gunning (partially hidden), Hollis Watkins, Guy Carawan, Florence Reece, Willie Peacock, Bob Zellner, Amanda Perdew, Pete Seeger, and Yasmeen Bheti Williams-Johnson, Aisha Kahlil, Evelyn Maria Harris, Bernice Johnson Reagon (all of *Sweet Honey in the Rock*) at Highlander's fiftieth anniversary concert, Knoxville, Tennessee, 1982. *Highlander. Deborah Barndt.*

When Highlander workshops are described to people who haven't experienced them, it often sounds like we are always contradicting ourselves, because we do things differently every time, according to what is needed. We've changed methods and techniques over the years, but the philosophy and conditions for learning stay the same. There is no method to learn from Highlander. What we do involves trusting people and believing in their ability to think for themselves. Our desire is to empower people collectively, not individually.

• • • •

Song, music and food are integral parts of education at Highlander. Music is one way for people to express their traditions, longings and determination. Many people have made significant contributions to music at Highlander. In the early days, Woody Guthrie and Pete Seeger came to visit. Later on, Frank Hamilton and Jack Elliott spent time with us. More recently, the Freedom Singers, Bernice Reagon and Sweet Honey in the Rock, as well as Highlander's former codirector, Jane Sapp, have been regular contributors. There were also those who stayed at Highlander for longer periods, such as Lee Hays, one of the original Almanac Singers, and Waldemar Hille.

The moving spirit in shaping the singing and music program at Highlander was my wife, Zilphia, who was active until her death in April 1956. One of the things she did was to revise and adapt songs so they could be used in the struggles Highlander was involved in. "We Will Overcome" was a song brought to Highlander from the picket line of the Charleston, South Carolina, American Tobacco Company strike in 1945. Originally it had been a religious song. Zilphia made some changes and used it as a union song. Later, Pete Seeger changed it to "We *Shall* Overcome." Then, in the 1960s, at a Highlander meeting of civil rights sit-in students, who eventually became the nucleus of SNCC, Guy Carawan encouraged everyone to contribute new words to the song. Guy had become a member of the Highlander staff at the recommendation of Pete Seeger, and he taught that song all over the South. He and his wife, Candie, carried on the Highlander tradition of using music as a central part of the social struggle. Other than encouraging others, I made no significant contributions to music at the school, unless you count the verse I added to "We Shall Overcome"—"The truth shall make us free."

Of all the things we considered in planning a workshop one of the most important was food. You can't have people coming to a residential situation and ask them to eat unfamiliar food, to adjust to new tastes, when the main task is to deal with their problems. We would never try to make people vegetarians, for example, or keep them from eating sweets, or try to make vegetarians eat meat—that's not why people came to Highlander. We never wanted to cover the waterfront.

When we had visitors like the Welsh miners, who came to meet with miners from Appalachia, we knew that working people in

Guy Carawan, Fannie Lou Hamer and Bernice Reagon at the New-port Folk Festival. *Joe Alper. Courtesy Jackie Gibson Alper.*

Wales could eat what working people in Appalachia eat. Nina Rein-ing, our cook, didn't know what Welsh food was, but she knew about good country eating. The food has to be as carefully thought out a part of the workshop as the music and the dance and the informal times when people can walk and talk and get to know each other better. Everything is integral. Even calling attention to the beautiful mountain view is part of it. We like to get out on the front porch so people can see the mountains and talk about them, and about the birds, flowers and rivers. And then, if people want

159

to talk about very serious things, they can walk in the woods. Residential workshops are a twenty-four-hour-a-day education.

Still, we never had enough room for leisure time during workshop sessions. Once, Highlander got so packed with things, so overwhelmed by energy, by people trying to cover so much and crowd the schedule, that I announced my desire for somebody to take over my union problems class. I told the students I wanted to have a new job, I wanted to be professor of leisure. My job would be to see that there were periods of leisure that nobody could encroach on. I would have an hour of leisure a day, and also be the policeman to make sure that everyone had time to do anything that pleased them during that hour.

Learning in society, outside school walls, takes place around the clock. It isn't restricted to specified times, certainly not to the same time of day for a limited number of minutes for, say, math, and then to another block of time for another subject. That's not life. Some of the best education at Highlander happened when the sessions were over: at meals, on walks, and when people went back to their dormitories and sat around drinking coffee or whatever else they brought.

THIRTEEN

Taking It Home

Highlander was involved in two major social movements—the industrial union movement, which was organized by the CIO, and the civil rights movement. They differed structurally but had in common a struggle for justice and human rights. The labor movement was based on local unions, which were much more than collective bargaining units. They provided a base for political and community activities, cultural and educational programs, and much more.

The civil rights movement was loosely organized, with no fixed structures on the local level to work through. The participants in the Citizenship Schools, voter registration, leadership, and other workshops at Highlander and throughout the South were recruited by staff and community volunteers.

We hoped that the organizations we were working with would move in a democratic direction and become part of a unified struggle for justice for all. Our role at Highlander was to provide a model of democratic functioning that people could incorporate into their own groups.

During the CIO times, we had the labor students run their own programs, except that on the first day of a session, we suggested that they follow the advice of the group that had come before them as to what they should do. Then they would be asked to do the same thing for the group to follow them. That first night we would get them together at a meeting, not unlike one they'd have in their own union. They would elect committees to take over all the responsibilities. We said that it was absolutely in their hands and that they would have to make all the decisions—curriculum decisions, discipline decisions, decisions about who was going to speak and what the topic would be. That was the way they would have to learn decision making, and taking responsibility for the programs. The Highlander staff had no veto power.

The people we were dealing with in the CIO period were practically all rank and file leaders, shop stewards, and local leaders from new unions in the South who didn't have any experience running unions. They had the same basic problems, and they were used to handling them through committees—that's how the unions did things—so this was the kind of program we had. The labor movement is structured in such a way that unions are run by committees. People are assigned to committees to put out a newspaper, negotiate, work on political action, or maybe work with the community.

Different things happened in the civil rights workshops. In those days we didn't have people with similar problems coming in together, so each group decided its own program, rather than beginning with an agenda set up by a preceding group, as was the case in the labor workshops. We didn't have people divide into committees, either, because committees weren't the way things worked in the civil rights movement. People in northern Mississippi operated differently from people in southern Mississippi or Alabama.

Myles Horton (left) welcoming oil worker at Highlander, 1947.
State Historical Society of Wisconsin.

163

CIO school, Highlander. Bill Elkus, back to camera, 1940s. *Highlander.*

They were all working for the same goal, but the procedures and situations varied. The civil rights movement was much more sporadic than the union movement, and we had to think in terms of how to deal with the nuances of particular problems and situations. We asked the people to make decisions the same way; they just didn't organize themselves the way the union members did.

The woman I met in Mississippi who started her own Citizenship School and was teaching other people to form theirs is a good illustration of this. She didn't know where the idea came from or that there was a whole network of schools all over the South. Even if you establish a pattern, people will work outside of it, and that's fine in a movement like the civil rights movement. People just do things on their own. There's a lot of spontaneity in a movement, and this quality is its genius—many, many people are energized to become active. People coalesce around certain events like demonstrations or voter registration campaigns. But in between they're doing their own thing; they're doing whatever they want to do, and it comes together because it is under the tent of fighting for civil rights.

Nonstructured social movements like the civil rights movement are exciting and dynamic and difficult to design an educational program for. Although we did do formal educational programs for SCLC and SNCC they were not like the ones we did with unions. In the last years of the labor period, rather than training the union members ourselves, we spent most of our time teaching people how to do labor education. We ended up having five southern states with Highlander-trained CIO state educational directors, and in the majority of the CIO unions operating in the South, Highlander-trained people were running the educational programs for the unions.

Right now we're going through an organizational period, and have been since the end of the civil rights movement. As far as the South is concerned, the antiwar movement didn't affect the program at Highlander as much as it did the universities and cities, because we worked primarily with nonschooled adults. We've been primarily in an organizational stage since the Poor People's Campaign during the 1960s. It didn't produce the multiracial coalition of disadvantaged groups we had hoped for. Ever since, we've been working in what I call "the valley," which is my name for this organizational period. The peak period is the social movement period.

What we did during the civil rights period was to develop or locate in most cases local community leaders to run workshops. When approached to do a workshop in, say, Mississippi or Alabama, we would first ask some of the people who were interested in education among the community leadership to assist us with the workshop. Gradually we would turn its operation over to them. By the time we had begun to withdraw our educational leadership from the civil rights movement, we were having workshops in which the full responsibility was shared by the participants, even though these workshops were Highlander-financed. We put local civil rights leaders and community people on our staff temporarily to run the workshops.

When the Mississippi Freedom Summer of 1965 was in the planning stage, Bob Moses asked us to do a workshop, and I told him, "Bob, you know that I've said we're not going to run any more workshops because you've got plenty of leadership that we've already worked with. They know what we know. We'll cooperate with them, and we'll finance and sponsor it. We'll do anything, but we're not going to take the responsibility for running it."

"Just make an exception this one last time," he said, "because this is important."

I said, "No, you can't keep making exceptions. If you want that workshop, you'll have to take the responsibility. I'll be down there, but you'll have to run it."

Bob said, "Well, I can't do it myself because I have to be somewhere else, but I'll get some other people to do it. If that's your condition, we'll do it." This turned out to be one of SNCC's most important workshops.

More recently, thirty black and white West Virginia welfare recipients from a rural Boone County coal mining community approached us with a request for a workshop on organizing. These women had either been to Highlander or heard about it, and they wanted to discuss community education and strategies for setting up their own welfare rights organization. The group had broken away from the National Welfare Rights Organization when the national people told them that their job was to support the national office and not to do things on their own. The organization at the state level had almost no leadership and was primarily concerned with getting legislative programs passed in Congress.

That is a legitimate thing for an organization to do, but it wasn't what the West Virginia people wanted, so they pulled away, already knowing they wanted to set up a state organization to work on issues important to them as well as national issues. They hoped Highlander could help them figure out how to get the state organization going.

The group came to Highlander and spent four days talking about their experiences of being on welfare and about the kinds of things that would make welfare programs more effective. They wanted to know how to deal with welfare snoopers, how to organize welfare workers and recipients. At the end of the workshop they decided they could go home and create an independent welfare rights group by using their own workshops as an organizing strategy.

During the sessions we talked about the process of running workshops, including what you had to watch for to keep the process going. I reminded them that when one of the women began to talk too much yesterday, I had had to figure out a way to quiet her down. I told them exactly how I went about doing it. Everything they asked about I tried to tell them from my point of view as workshop leader and member of the circle of learning. I also had to tell them that what they were trying to do was going to be hard, and how easy it is to lose your nerve in the middle of a struggle. I said that here at Highlander during the workshop, we had everybody together. "We all love each other, and we're all fighting together for the same purpose, and you can succeed if you nurture each other. But you don't know that you've learned anything until you've demonstrated that you can pass it on, and to pass it on you have to know it. To think that you know it is not proof that you do. Since this is so important, let's do role playing, just as if you were already back in West Virginia."

For a day and a half, people took turns playing different roles: welfare workers, welfare clients, politicians. People took as much time as they wanted to practice what they would do when they got home, and then they asked questions and practiced again.

At the last session I said to the group, "For your organization to work, you have to go home and do what we've done here. Each of you should run Highlander-type workshops, and then the people you train can run their own workshops. Just as in the Citizenship Schools, you do one workshop and train ten people, and then each one of them trains ten people so that they can replicate what they learned from you." At the Highlander workshop the group developed a strategy to build a welfare rights organization. They decided that an educational program was essential in order to explain to members their legal rights, and for them to understand the intricacies of the welfare laws in their state. The question of who should be the teachers came up, and the answer was the welfare recipients themselves. They knew the problem better than anyone else, so they would be the best teachers of their own people.

The women who attended the workshop returned to West Virginia and, through education, built an organization of close to a thousand members. They didn't have any organizers coming in from outside, and all but one of them fanned out through West Virginia to run workshops. They found lawyers who were willing to help interpret laws. Then they located university students and

167

VISTA volunteers to help supply transportation, research and public relations skills. Church organizations provided funds and some technical assistance.

As a result, there were many successes and their organization grew. They also kept in touch with Highlander, and every once in a while one of them would come to talk about specific problems. Three years after the workshop, the state of West Virginia was planning to revise the welfare code. People in the new welfare rights organization asked Highlander to put them in touch with officials from the states that had the best welfare codes and programs. Then these women held educational workshops all over the state to study welfare codes. By this time, they knew more about welfare laws than anyone else in the state, including the legislative committee that was set up to write them. When the legislature met to consider the new codes, the welfare rights organization asked to testify, and they were told to go home.

These women knew their business and they knew what was going to happen, so they said, "No, we're not going home. What we're going to do is get some more women here, and we'll stay until we can testify."

The legislative committee said they could stay until hell froze over, but that they would not be allowed to testify. The women insisted that if they couldn't testify, there would be no meeting of the legislature the next day, because they would bring in miners from their communities and close down the Capitol.

The next day miners started pouring in by the hundreds, and in no time the legislative committee invited the women to testify. They had their bill and a strategy, and the new law passed by the legislature included many ideas the welfare organization had formulated in its workshops.

This illustrates the role of education in extending democracy.

FOURTEEN

A Growing Idea

Democracy needs to be not only political but part of the fabric of society as a whole. When I use the word "democracy," it is not limited to political decision making, to voting. It is a philosophical concept meaning that people are really free and empowered to make collectively the decisions that affect their lives.

In a democracy there can't be individual decisions that run counter to the welfare of other people. Decisions about the quality of life, culture, entertainment, distribution of income have to be made collectively and not left up to money-making interests. The people

169

are the only ones who should make these decisions, not input from poor people who need low-cost housing and education loans. They might make some bad ones, but the opportunity should be theirs.

As it is now, advertisers make the decisions about the media, not the people, because the media exist for the purpose of making money. The bottom line determines a bank's decisions, not input from poor people who need low-cost housing and education loans. People have no access.

This is true of voting. Ronald Reagan was elected by less than 30 percent of the eligible voters each time he ran. Our system doesn't require equal participation; it can function politically with the participation of only a minority of the people who are qualified to vote. There would be nothing illegal about 5 percent of the population electing a president.

Our whole system was built on the idea that there were limits to voting: women have only been able to vote since 1920; until very recently, young people had to wait until they were twenty-one to vote; and up until the civil rights movement, people had to pass a literacy test in most of the South before they could vote. Until the civil rights movement, there were a lot of ways to keep people from voting. Only well-to-do white males twenty-one or over have never had to face restrictions.

The fact that people with money can hire lobbyists to represent them in Washington limits equity in the political system. Poor people don't have the money for this—if they spent everything they had, they couldn't get enough money together to equal the lobbying power of the rich. After an election, people don't have access to government, because lack of money prevents them from having equal access to the people in power. That's an inequity that's built into the system. That's where money is more powerful than people.

People do have a right to vote. But whom do they have a right to vote for? They have a right to vote for whoever is chosen. That's our dilemma right now. It starts with how much it costs to run for office—it now costs $3 million to run for governor in Tennessee. That rules out a lot of people. So the choice is between two people who are willing to spend $3 million, which is not a democratic choice. You can say that the people have a right to vote, but they only have the right to choose between two millionaires or people whom other people with money are willing to back.

170

I don't have a static definition of democracy. My conception of democracy has changed and grown. What I thought democracy was fifty years ago was probably true as far as it went, but my understanding was limited. When I first tried to learn about the nature of society, back before Highlander was started, I assumed that capitalism operated more or less within the boundaries of individual nations, and that if you could find a way to get a majority of the people to make the right decisions within that national framework, you could change a government to a more democratic form. I didn't realize then that capitalism would take a global form, in which the loyalties of transnational companies are to maximizing profits instead of to national interests. Even if we could get the majority of the people in the United States to pass laws or set up the kind of government that would deal nationally with capitalism, this move would only be partly effective, because capitalism is international. In recent years, companies take their tax rebates, close down plants and relocate whenever they think the controls on their environmental or employee policies interfere with their profits. They have no national loyalty, they have money loyalty, and you have to learn to deal internationally with economic problems.

What I understand now is that you can have democracy in voting, democracy in the workplace and a democratically chosen union, but unless you deal with world capitalism—transnationalism—the decisions you make are going to be very limited. Fundamental decisions aren't made by the politicians and officials of this country, they're made by the military-industrial complex. As long as that's true, there can be no democracy; there can be democratic processes, frameworks and things like that, but there can be no real democracy, because you aren't allowed to make decisions concerning what is most important.

There's another thing I didn't understand. I didn't foresee that when a crisis developed and the people began to rebel to ease the situation, some strategic concessions would be made to modify capitalism so that, at least temporarily, it wasn't so oppressive. There was more flexibility than I realized. I learned that from Roosevelt. He forced the capitalists to take the bitter pill of wiping out sweatshops and forced them to recognize unions so that capitalism could get well. He just forced it down their throats and put the capitalist system back on its feet. I didn't realize capitalism would yield to that kind of pressure.

I also hadn't realized that for democracy to be truly effective, it had to penetrate all parts of people's lives, providing them with a say about everything that was affecting them. I thought that things would be done by the government more than they are now. I think you have to have democracy right down into the home and into children's lives. It's got to be everywhere, but I didn't have that kind of understanding then. I still don't completely see the form democracy should take.

I've come to the conclusion that piecemeal democracy is not going to be sufficiently democratic, because when it gets stopped at any place, you get what's happening now to the gains made by the civil rights movement. Just consider the recent U.S. Supreme Court decisions on affirmative action. You lose the gains you made if you don't keep struggling.

There ought to be ways for people to have access to decision making. A good example of what I mean can be found in Sweden. The workers in some of the automobile plants not only have control of what jobs they do—and they can switch from one job to another—but they also have a say in the management of the plants, including how the profits will be distributed. There's a movement in some U.S. plants to give workers more democracy, but they don't have anything to say about the profits.

In this country we accept a system which assumes that people's lives, the natural resources and everything else exist for the purpose of making money. If you're going to kill off nature in the process of making money, that's too bad. And if it costs too much to alleviate environmental destruction and limit the depletion of natural resources, that's too bad also. Interestingly enough, Adam Smith, the father of capitalism, said in *The Wealth of Nations* that social costs should be part of the cost of making profits. In my lifetime, I haven't heard any capitalist say that. It's "We make money, we'll pollute, that's the public's problem."

Although democracy is limited by capitalism, some of its elements are strong in this country. We have more of a tradition of freedom of speech than any other country. It's not only a part of our dream, it's part of our reality. Sometimes we have to fight to protect this freedom.

Many years ago Martin Luther King, Jr., Fred Shuttlesworth, who was the president of the Alabama Christian Movement for Human Rights and a cofounder of SCLC, and I initiated a petition defending Robert Shelton, then head of the Ku Klux Klan in Alabama, for not giving his list of contributors and members to the FBI. We got hundreds of signatures saying that the FBI had no right to force him to do that. Our help certainly wasn't appreciated by Shelton or the Klan. In fact, when Shelton was questioned publicly about it, he said he didn't ask us to help, didn't accept that kind of support and wished to hell we'd kept out of it. He said it was none of our business, and that if he had to build support like us, he'd rather not have any. The press asked me what my reaction was, and I said that we didn't support Shelton for his benefit. We did it because we believe in the principle of freedom of expression. It could be us next time. The FBI had already demanded Highlander's list and I'd refused to give it to them. That's the principle: if King and Shuttlesworth and I defended it for ourselves, then we had to defend it for our enemies. The Klan was our enemy—hell, there's nobody who was a worse enemy to the three of us than that guy—but it was a matter of principle.

The same thing happened when the Klan wanted to have a march in front of Highlander while we were in Knoxville. I didn't object or try to stop them. I told the press and the mayor, "They have a right to march, as long as they stay on the public streets. We defend their right to march past Highlander."

What we did, though, was to invite all the black neighbors and all the white friends of Highlander in Knoxville to come for a picnic on the Highlander lawn and watch the parade. We had seven or eight hundred people there, and we had a hundred kids playing right down by the road, and off-duty black policemen volunteered to come out to see that none of the Klan people got on our land or parked their cars there. The chief of police had told them to take a vacation that day because he didn't want them near the parade. They didn't wear their uniforms, but they had their guns strapped around them, which they were allowed to do.

The Klan was humiliated, because we turned the purpose of their march around and made fun of it instead of letting them intimidate us. They looked very embarrassed as they went by, and although they were supposed to march back again, they took another route to avoid having to deal with that crowd jeering and making fun of them.

I don't know what I'd have done if I'd been in Skokie, Illinois, when the Nazi party tried to march through the Jewish community, but I think I might have suggested that the people in Skokie, by the thousands, make a line on both sides of the marchers, bar the media from covering the event and stand there in stony silence, letting them march.

There are ways to deal with these kinds of demonstrations other than banning them. We've got to preserve the right to demonstrate and to speak because you can never change society if the doors of discussion are closed. You don't ever want to set the precedent of banning freedom of expression. We in the United States know what freedom is because this country was born in a struggle for freedom. The American Civil Liberties Union exists to keep freedom of speech alive. Some antidemocratic interests have been trying to put Highlander out of business for fifty years and haven't succeeded, because of the degree of our freedom of speech. We couldn't have survived if there was none. And that's in a capitalist society getting more capitalist all the time. I've spent my entire life trying to extend democracy in capitalism. It's the only place I've ever worked.

To have democracy, you must have a society in which decision making is real, and that means replacing, transforming and rebuilding society so as to allow for people to make decisions that affect their lives. These decisions shouldn't be counteracted by an economic structure in which maximizing profits overrides all other values. It's a growing concept that has to do with moving in a certain direction. All you can talk about is the direction and some of the elements you want to see built into the kind of society that you don't have now but would like to see in the future. But as you move toward it, you may notice lots of weaknesses and limitations in your concepts, so you change them. This is why I've never been able to define democracy. Somebody once said of me that I purposely refuse to state what I mean by democracy. As if it were secret. It's just that for me, it's a growing idea.

FIFTEEN

One Battle, Many Fronts

Any educational philosophy comes out of what you do and how you deal with people. When you believe in people and in the importance of trying to create a democracy, you must turn these beliefs into practice, and if you don't believe in the free enterprise system and individual competitiveness, you practice group action and cooperation. You practice learning in groups so that people can learn to solve problems through group action.

This type of educational work involves a different way of working with people than community or labor organizers use. I've always taken the position that Highlander was not in the business of organizing, or even of training organizers, but in education for action, and in helping to develop social leadership.

A few years ago the singer and activist "Utah" Phillips gave me a little pin that says, "One Battle, Many Fronts." The one battle is to rebuild this country, but there are many fronts for dealing with revolutionary change. Instead of saying, "We are going to organize," we say, "Our job is to help people who may become organizers." We try to develop people's ability to analyze, to understand problems so that they can develop into organizers or other types of leaders.

A lot of people who have been to Highlander have become organizers. But we didn't say to them, "One, two, three. This is the way you organize a community project or a union." We tried to help them understand how to analyze their problem and the situation, and to get them committed philosophically to working for a more humane and just society. The advantage to our approach is that we don't get tied up in a specific organizing campaign with a limited goal.

There's a lot to be learned from successful organization over a specific issue, from achieving a specific victory, like preventing a building from being torn down or getting a new sewer system. However, some equally valuable learning takes place when you escalate your demands to the place where you finally lose. Now if you don't push to the place where you might fail, you've missed a wonderful opportunity to learn to struggle, to think big and challenge the status quo, and also to learn how to deal with failure. If you analyze them, you can learn more in some ways from failures than from successes. Now, all this is predicated on learning from analyzing your experience. An experience you don't learn from is just a happening.

I've always thought it was important to persuade people to be willing to fail because if you're not willing to fail, you'll always choose easy goals and learn from that to continue to choose easy goals. Your sights are limited by what you do. The pursuit of an expanding, unrestricted goal that is always receding in front of you, as you get a clearer view of where you're going or would like to, is not an experience to shun. The opposite experience occurs when the goal is a limited reform, or some easily attained thing. I don't agree with those who believe in designing a program primarily so that people will have an experience of winning.

This is a major difference between me and many people who claim to be Saul Alinsky-type organizers. Saul himself, when he said that you must have victories, was talking about a victory that they wouldn't even dare tackle. He was referring to the taking of Chicago's South Side, and as he said, "Rubbing raw the sores of discontent," by using the people at the bottom—the dispossessed, the poor—to force the rich, the property-owning church, and the bankers to make changes that would keep the area from destroying itself. And he succeeded in doing that. That kind of success is important. You learn that you can tackle big jobs and you learn how to succeed.

I met Saul in the 1940s when he was organizing the Back of the Yards with the Packinghouse Workers. I was familiar with the conditions in the slaughterhouses through Upton Sinclair's book *The Jungle*, and that's about all I knew concerning them. I hadn't come in contact with Saul when I was at the University of Chicago, so when I later found out about the organizing community there, I made a point to learn more.

Saul was supremely self-confident. That was part of his strength—he was strong enough that nobody could intimidate him. As he developed in his organizing, he became one of Highlander's best fund-raisers in Chicago. Saul and Studs Terkel took turns making fund-raising speeches. Usually I'd go up and tell some stories about what was going on at Highlander. There's a famous one about what happened when we were working with the Farmers Union in the 1950s in southern Alabama. We'd brought blacks and whites together at Highlander to exchange experiences and to set up a fertilizer cooperative with black and white directors. Since we had to carry the conservative white farmers along with us, we had to build a strong support group, and we had to deal with racism and get political support to survive. J. D. Mott, a white Alabama farmer who became a co-op leader, was very clever at helping his neighbors accept blacks, and he knew he had to deal with some of the symbols of racism like not eating or drinking together. He was also intuitive enough to know you couldn't tackle such an enormous problem from a rational basis alone.

One of the stories I liked to tell had to do with Highlander's attempts to build these co-ops. In southern Alabama it gets so hot that the workers would always drink lots of ice water. They'd consume gallons and gallons, so there would always be a big hunk of ice in a barrel of water, and next to it they'd hang what they called a colored dipper and a white dipper. J. D. Mott decided he'd take advantage of that situation and do a little education, and so he took the white dipper away. These thirsty white farmers came to get a drink and couldn't find their dipper. When they'd look around and not see anybody there, they'd take the colored dipper and drink from it. Mott was off where he could watch them. He'd see them hesitate a while, trying to figure how to get their heads down to drink from the barrel. It would be too difficult, and they'd finally say, "What the hell, I'll take the colored dipper and use it before anybody sees me." In a few days everyone was drinking out of the same dipper.

We were always glad to get the people accustomed to moving away from social symbols of segregation. I'd use this story when I wanted to tell people how Highlander went about doing education. Then one time when I was getting ready to speak at a Highlander fund-raiser in Chicago, Saul said, "If you tell that goddamned dipper story again I'm going to walk out." He never pulled any punches about what he wanted to say either to his friends or enemies.

I have great resentment today toward some of the people who trade on Saul Alinsky's name and train organizers by what they call the Alinsky Method, when it is often only mechanically and technically Alinsky's. They think it's a matter of gimmicks. What made him such a good organizer was his tremendous sense of humor, his brilliance and his utter disregard for what anybody said about him. He could have organized in half a dozen different ways and it would have worked, though some people think it was the particular method that was responsible. You don't try to imitate people who know more than you. You try to learn from them. If he had to use pressure, he'd try to mix a little fun in with it. Once, for example, when he was organizing on the South Side of Chicago, they were having trouble because no one was hauling away the garbage in a black neighborhood. The man in charge of garbage removal was unapproachable. Finally, the people Saul was organizing loaded up some trucks with garbage and dumped it on the front lawn of the official's North Shore mansion. Then they waited across the street until he came home so they could see his reaction. Most organizers would have gone home, but Saul knew that part of it was having the fun of seeing him deal with their garbage. The very next day all the garbage was removed from the black neighborhood.

Another time, Saul's organization was trying to get something done about the South Side schools. The chairman of the school board was the president of a bank. Since they couldn't put pressure on him as chairman of the board, Saul decided there was only one way to get his attention. They organized a day of picnics and celebration down in the Loop in front of his bank, and way before the bank opened, there were long lines of picnicking people waiting to enter. Later, they all went in and opened accounts. It took hours. Nobody else could get in, but the bank people couldn't call the police to stop them because they had taken out advertisements encouraging new business. Then, when everybody had opened accounts, they came back and withdrew their money. By now it was the middle of the afternoon. All the time they were doing this, there were people singing and dancing and picnicking outside. Saul managed to inject a little fun into his programs when it was appropriate. That's clever organizing.

Saul wanted to start a movement. In his book *Reveille for Radicals*, he writes about gathering people to organize communities from the bottom up. His organizers would get the people all stirred up, and they would develop their own leadership. He would start with one of the immediate problems, a step that leads to a long-range goal. Too often, however, his imitators have translated that to mean it's important to win the smallest victory without necessarily making any connection with the long-range goal. They seem to think that if you tell people there's a difficult long-range goal, they'll be too discouraged even to begin working toward it.

Most of the time, Saul was extremely successful in getting people empowered to provide their own leadership. He also believed that these leaders would be so imbued with the idea of poor people's power that they'd want to go out and organize other communities. He thought they'd want to share what they had learned with other people and that there would be a radical community movement. He felt this movement would spread, but it didn't, because once the local leaders he had developed got into power, they held on to it and stayed where they were. In the Back of the Yards community in Chicago, the people Saul had worked with became part of a racist power structure. This was the first community Saul had organized, and he was very upset about the outcome. He used to talk to me about finding a way to prevent this from happening again. He was not just an organizer for anything, he had real principles, and he would do anything to stick to them and win out. There was no way anybody could get at him by threatening him.

Although I always had tremendous respect for his integrity and ability, I didn't always agree with Saul. His purpose was to put the poor and disinherited in power. He didn't realize that when these people were no longer poor themselves, they wouldn't necessarily be dedicated to poor people anymore.

Saul and I differed because my position was that if I had to make a choice between achieving an objective and utilizing the struggle to develop and radicalize people, my choice would be to let the goal go and develop the people. He believed that organizing success was the way to radicalize people. We were both trying to do the same thing, but we differed in method. When I look at a situation in order to decide whether to work with an organization, it's essential to consider whether that organization is moving toward structural reform or limited reform. If it's moving toward structural reform, I'll work with that organization. If it's just limited reform, I would hesitate, because I don't think valuable learning comes out of winning little victories, unless they are calculated steps toward the large goal and will lead to structural reforms.

A young organizer once told me about how he had to organize under pressure and didn't have time to educate people. "We are in competition with other organizations for funds," he said. "We have to organize fast to get them, because if our competition organizes faster than we can, then they get the funds."

Instead of having a chance to involve the people and educating them, the organizers would just pull the people together long enough to get the privilege of speaking for them, and then they'd go down to the city council and say, "I represent two hundred people," instead of having the people do it themselves, which would take a longer time. They'd tell me, "If we took time to do what you suggest, somebody else who didn't take that time would get the record of having organized faster and better, and they'd get the funds." Winning a victory doesn't necessarily educate anybody to do anything or follow it up. It just gets that specific thing done and then the organization falls apart. In terms of the effect the victory has on society, it's the same as knowing an official or some friend of an official and getting him to do it. People should be helped to understand that they don't have to depend on favors from people who have power.

If you're not committed to radical education, you may be able to justify achieving specific aims that may benefit people without involving them in the process. They don't learn anything, but they get something by authorizing you to speak on their behalf.

There are a lot of combinations in which they work together, but when the crunch comes, you may have to make a decision as to whether you want to achieve an organizational goal or develop people's thinking. I can recall two experiences having to do with organization in which people decided they didn't want to do what they set out to accomplish. From an organizing point of view, that's a bad record, because the organizers didn't achieve their goal.

In a neighboring county during the 1940s, people at Highlander were working with the farmers, trying to put together a state political coalition. The University of Tennessee had a man in Extension who was responsible for organizing co-ops. Whether they finally succeeded or failed, he got credit for setting them up. He told the farmers they should have a dairy co-op. There was a Farmers Union local over there, and they asked us to organize a dairy co-op for them. We said, "No no, you've got to organize it. We'll help you, but you organize it. Let's get some facts. How many people will be in it? How much milk is there?" and so on. They said, "The university will send out a questionnaire." And we said, "No no, you talk to the people or telephone them or something. Make personal contact."

We wanted them to get to know each other and work together. They gathered all the facts: how many cows there were, how much milk there was, and so on. They did all the work. And we said, "OK, now is that enough for a successful dairy co-op? Is that enough volume to make an efficient production unit?" They didn't know. We said we didn't either, but I added, "I have a friend in another Farmers Union local who runs a dairy co-op, and we can ask him." He provided the facts and figures that showed there wasn't enough volume to have a co-op.

When this guy from the university extension found out about it, he raised hell because we had killed his chance of organizing a dairy co-op. But the people learned a lot in the process. They saved themselves a lot of money and a lot of headaches because they learned the facts. They made an analysis themselves. That wasn't a very good organizing job, but it was a good educational job.

Another instance occurred with the labor unions in Knoxville, Tennessee. They had a big textile strike, and they wanted some classes so they could learn about unions while they were out. We recruited teaching volunteers. In the morning they worked in offices and businesses, so we set up some classes at 6:00 A.M. and held others at night. There were about six picket posts, and we had two classes a day at each one.

During those classes people wanted to discuss how the contract worked and what the demands were. One of the conclusions they came to was that their demands were not justified. They'd gotten all excited and struck over something that wasn't in their contract. They were saying, "It's in the contract," and they found it wasn't. So they were in a quandary.

They got together at a meeting and discussed the situation. They said, "Well, we can't tell the company we were wrong. We've got a lot of solidarity and spirit here. Let's think of something else to demand." They didn't go back to work, they just kept the picket line and made another demand, which they won. But they dropped the first demand because they learned they were wrong. It didn't break the union; it didn't break the strike. In fact, it strengthened the union. As an organizing strategy you would never do such a thing. But we trust people to be intelligent and capable of learning. That's not organizing, that's education.

If you're interested in accomplishing something small but very important to the people in a neighborhood—like dealing with a building that's run down—and your goal is either to get rid of that building or to improve it so that it's livable, then you aren't concerned about whether you get it done by going to the politicians and promising you'll vote for them next time, or by finding the guy who owns it and convincing him that he can make more money if he turns it into an apartment house, or by demonstrating and protesting and embarrassing the city. You don't care which of those methods you use as long as your objective is achieved. An organizer, in that situation, might very well have said to the people, "Don't say anything, just get a little committee and go to the ward heeler here and help him, get him interested and promise him your support, and get him to do it quietly. If you go out and demonstrate and start yelling, you'll interfere, so keep your mouths shut." And the ward heeler would take care of the building, and it would help the community because that building shouldn't be there. The goal would be a worthwhile social one, but no learning would take place, because the organizer's strategy was designed not to help people learn to do things for themselves, but to achieve that goal. In a situation like that I'd think, "This is a good opportunity to educate people, for people to become educated as to what they can do with their power, and how they can do things by using people power." I'd try to create a crisis, using it as another part of the education, in which people would learn to deal with opposition and to work through it. When I was done, if I had succeeded, the people would have both a good building and a lot of strength. If I had to make a choice, I'd let the building go and develop the people.

It's dangerous to do this kind of education, to push the boundaries to the place where people might be fired or get in some other kind of trouble. But you've got to get on that line, as close as you possibly can, and sometimes you'll analyze it wrong and get clipped. If people don't take chances, they'll never keep pushing. They must explore and push as far as they can. People get the exhilaration of liberating themselves, pushing that boundary line until they push it to the place where they're challenged, and they either have to back off or go further, so they just say, "I'd rather lose my job than not do what I want to do. I'll push until I lose my job, because I'd rather lose the job than be boxed in."

Quite often this process leads to an examination of why they are in the box anyway. And often they go beyond that and do get fired, get in trouble, but here's the interesting thing: there are few people I've been involved with in pushing the boundary lines who got fired that don't thank me today for the role I played in getting them moving. Because by the time they do, they are liberated enough that they are not going to spend the rest of their lives boxed in, and of course most of the time they land on their feet. They get a better job, something they are more interested in. They don't die, they're not ostracized. I don't hesitate at all to get people to push out to the place where they get in trouble. Now, I hesitate to advise them to do it, but when they do it themselves, I think it's fine.

I tell people it might be painful, that they might go hungry, they might have problems with their families. I don't mislead people. They arrive at the point where they want to talk about the rough times ahead; they begin to speculate about what could happen. They've got to do it, they just have to talk it out. At that point I say, "Look, it's fine. I'm not going to tell anybody to slow down in liberating themselves, but you have to know what the price might be, that these are some of the things that have happened." And I tell them what's happened to other people. Often they say, "You know, I'll do it anyway."

I don't think you help people by keeping them enslaved to something that is less than they are capable of doing and believing. I was told one time during an educational conference that I was cruel because I made people who were very happy and contented, unhappy, and that it was wrong to upset people and stretch their imaginations and minds, and to challenge them to the place where they got themselves into trouble, became maladjusted and so on. My position was that I believed in changing society by first changing individuals, so that they could then struggle to bring about social changes. There's a lot of pain in it, and a lot of violence, and conflict, and that is just part of the price you pay. I realized that was part of growth—and growth is painful. A plant comes through the hard ground, and it breaks the seed apart. And then it dies to live again.

I think that people aren't fully free until they're in a struggle for justice. And that means for everyone. It's a struggle of such importance that they are willing, if necessary, to die for it. I think that's what you have to do before you're really free. Then you've got something to live for. You don't want to die, because you've got so much you want to do. This struggle is so important that it gives a meaning to life. Now that sounds like a contradiction, but I encourage people to push limits, to try to take that step, because that's when they are really free. I saw this happen during the time of the sit-ins and the formation of the Student Nonviolent Coordinating Committee.

SNCC grew out of the student sit-ins in the traditionally black colleges of the South. The sit-ins began in Greensboro and then spread to Nashville, Atlanta and elsewhere. Students started protesting at the lunch counters of stores where they bought their clothes and school supplies, and in theaters and other public places. For a number of years before the student sit-ins, Highlander had been holding four-day workshops for high school and college stu-

Highlander workshop for SNCC, Knoxville, Tennessee, 1962. Charles Jones speaking, center. *Highlander.*

dents over Easter weekend. They were primarily for black students, but white students came too. The students ran them themselves. They decided what they wanted to do and whom they wanted there as consultants and advisors. Each year they'd plan their future programs in advance. They'd talk about interracial dating and fraternities, college exchange students and things like that.

Most of these students had first come to Highlander with their parents, who were so pleased to find a place where social equality was practiced—where you could swim in the lake, eat and picnic together—that they wanted their kids to come also, to learn that there were some decent white people.

The parents were leaders in their communities, people who had to make decisions and act on them. They talked out of their experience. The students were into book learning. Whenever they'd try to participate in one of their parents' workshops, they'd remember something they'd read in a sociology class or psychology class and they'd say, "Well, why don't you do this?"—right out of a book. The parents thought it was brilliant; they were so pleased

185

to have these bright kids talking about all the things they were learning in school that had absolutely nothing to do with the situation we were talking about. I finally said, "Look, we've got to talk about serious business. I appreciate all your erudition, all your knowledge and contributions, but maybe we'd better let the people who are going to be back home taking care of this problem discuss it, because they're the ones who are going to have to work it out." The students didn't like this at all. They said, "You're not fair to us. This is the only place like this we can go to in the South."

I had to tell them that Highlander is for out-of-school adults. "If you had graduated and were outside the schooling system and involved in a community organization, it would be different. What we can do, though, is run a four-day workshop for you every year. You can run it any way you please, but until you get out in the community, it's not going to be part of the adult program."

In the meantime they started sitting down and getting put in jail, and when they came back to Highlander they said, "Ha. Now, we've been out in the community; we've done a lot of things out of school. What are you going to do about it? Are we adults?" I said, "Well, from now on, anybody that's been in jail is an adult."

At that meeting they discussed how they could link up. Should they organize? Should they be part of the NAACP or the Southern Christian Leadership Conference? The forty students who were there decided that they wanted to work together but stay independent of other groups.

The rest of the discussion was on nonviolence. Four or five of the people there, including John Lewis, had learned about nonviolence and were interested in it from a religious or philosophical point, but the rest of the students agreed it was important they just accept it as a tactic.

Less than a month later, SCLC invited them to come to a meeting at Shaw University in North Carolina. Fortunately for the future, Ella Baker, a very intelligent and wise woman who had been working in the South for years for the NAACP and SCLC, was attending this meeting, and she just gathered them all up. When they told her they wanted to have a separate organization, she helped them set up one. She stayed with the students as a kind of advisor, but they were basically on their own. The organization that resulted was SNCC, which played a much more militant and grassroots role than SCLC, which was run by black ministers.

186

When the students first started the sit-ins, their parents had told them to stay out of jail. "It'll disgrace the family, it'll disgrace you and you'll get it on your record. We worked hard to send you to college." But the students had other ideas. They got carried away with the idea of picketing Woolworths because they bought a lot of their things there and yet weren't allowed to drink or eat at the lunch counter. So they got together—Candie Carawan, later a Highlander staff member, was one of them, the first white woman arrested in the student sit-ins during the civil rights movement— and they went down, laughing and talking, to show these white folks. It never occurred to them that they'd go to jail. They hadn't gotten that far. They were locked up that night, and after the first shock they started singing, and they kept on singing and bantering and laughing, the girls on one side of the jail and the boys on the other. But several of the kids' parents started calling me. "What's happening, our kids are in jail, it's disgraceful, what happened, do you know anything about this?"

They were terribly upset because they were socialized to think that going to jail was bad. But they got used to it, both the parents and the young people. The next thing the kids got used to was getting the hell beaten out of them. They were beginning to grow up, get liberated. Then they started marching. There was supposed to be a bus ride into Jackson, Mississippi, and it was canceled when people got beat up and it was decided to march instead of ride. The SNCC people—John Lewis, Diane Bevell, Charles Sherrod and then some of the others—said, "We can't stop. We've got to carry on. If we give up now, then it's over. They can't stop us, and we've got to be willing to pay whatever price." At that time, they made a commitment to die if necessary. John Lewis almost did when they beat him to a pulp, but that's when they declared their independence, that's when they became free. If you aren't afraid to die for your cause, then nobody can get at you. Nobody can push you around: jail won't do it, harassment won't do it, beatings won't do it, death won't do it, so you're home free. There isn't anything anybody can do to you but kill you. That's what liberation is, being willing to die for what you believe in. I practice it myself, and I advocate it for other people.

Living when you don't really live is no great shakes. If you're afraid to die, then you're afraid to live. So you don't really live if you're not free.

Eleanor Roosevelt speaking at Highlander. *Highlander*.

Now if you're free you aren't afraid to learn from everybody and anybody. Educators who disregard what you can learn from Marxism, for instance, are selling short the people they're trying to teach. Once the FBI came down and made a list of the Marxist books at Highlander, and they gave the information to the Birch Society. I had helped the FBI make that list. I had gone to the card file and said, "Here, copy them down." I later learned that the Birch Society's list was in the same order as the FBI's. It doesn't take much imagination to know where they got the list. Anyway, in it there were anti-Communist books, including ones by Birchers, as well as books by Trotsky and many other Communist writers. As long as a book had the word "Communist" in the title, it got lumped together with all the others.

Once at a meeting in Chattanooga, Tennessee, where Eleanor Roosevelt, Frank Graham (then president of the University of North Carolina) and I were speakers, the American Legion came in and protested my being on the program and tried to stop it. Somebody who'd seen this list of Communist books at our school got up and said, "Is it true or not true that you have these books at Highlander?" I told them it was true. "There've been good books written on Marxism and communism. And since that list was made we've got quite a few more." And he said, "I just wanted you to admit that it's a Communist school." He thought that was cute. I didn't say a word, I just gave him the information that we had more than he thought we had. Then Frank Graham got up. "Let me answer that question," he said. "You know, Myles doesn't claim that Highlander is an institution of higher learning, a university, or anything like that. It's a people's school, for working people. He respects them, and I respect them. I want to make it clear that any institution that claims to educate people should have sources that they can look at, either for or against, and I'm appalled at that list. At the University of North Carolina we've got several hundred times more books on communism, and, if anything, I think Highlander needs more books on communism." He thought something was wrong with us. It just brought down the house. We didn't have enough books. He had a wonderful sense of humor. Mrs. Roosevelt was back there chuckling.

One time Rosa Parks was in New York at the same time I happened to be there. The NAACP had sent her to a big meeting, and afterward they ignored her. They were going to pay for her hotel room, but nobody was doing anything else for her. I found out about it and called her up and asked her if there was anyone she would like to meet in New York. She told me she'd like to meet Eleanor Roosevelt and Ralph Bunche. (He was under secretary general of the United Nations at that time.)

"Well, Rosa, they're both good friends of mine and they'd be honored to meet you." So I called Mrs. Roosevelt and I told her that Rosa Parks was there.

Right away Mrs. Roosevelt asked, "When can I meet her?" and we arranged to have tea at her house.

189

When we got there I introduced them by saying, "It's a pleasure to be privileged to introduce the first lady of the land to the first lady of the South." That's the way I thought about them, and that's how I introduced them. Well, Mrs. Roosevelt asked her about being at Highlander, and what she'd done in Montgomery, and then she asked, "Have you been called a Communist yet, Mrs. Parks?" When Rosa answered yes, Mrs. Roosevelt said, "I suppose Myles told you when you were at Highlander that you'd be called a Communist." Rosa told her I hadn't warned her, and Mrs. Roosevelt criticized me for not telling her. I said, "If I'd known what she was going to do, I'd have told her. But when she was at Highlander, she said she wasn't going to do anything. She said that she came from the cradle of the Confederacy, and the white people wouldn't let the black people do anything, and besides, the black people hadn't been willing to stick together, so she didn't think she'd do anything. I didn't see any reason to tell a person who wasn't going to do anything that she'd be branded as a Communist because I knew she'd never be called a Communist if she didn't do anything. If I'd known she was going to start the civil rights movement, I'd have told her." And Rosa said, "Yes, he told me later on, after I got arrested." I did, I went down and I talked to her because I knew she was going to get it. Mrs. Roosevelt was so down-to-earth and practical; no fuss and feathers about her.

Franklin D. was different. He never got beyond a kind of political use of working people, and he didn't have an understanding of class problems. Mrs. Roosevelt had empathy with poor people and working people, and when she was at Highlander she could talk to the people just as any of the rest of us could. Very few nonworking-class guests had this ability. Most would talk at the people or around them, but not directly to them, because they didn't know how. Mrs. Roosevelt, however, could just sit down and talk to people—black people, white people, poor people, mountain people—and get them to feel comfortable around her.

John Beecher was another person not afraid to take risks. The night the 1965 civil rights march from Selma to Montgomery ended, John and I and several other people were staying with Clifford and Virginia Durr. We were having dinner and getting more and more worried about the safety of the people returning to Selma from Montgomery. Although the National Guard protected the people during the march, after it was over they disappeared. There was

Integration workshop, 1958. Myles Horton, Eleanor Roosevelt, James Stokely. *Highlander.*

no protection for the people who were going back to Selma from Montgomery, and we thought that it was an open invitation to the Klan to kill anyone they wanted to, now that all the cameras and reporters had gone home. While we were talking, we got a message that a woman, Viola Liuzzo, had been killed. John Beecher, who was a stringer for the *San Francisco Chronicle*, got on the phone and called the sheriff in Selma to get some more information about the killing. The sheriff said he didn't know anything about it, so John called the head of the National Guard and then two or three other people, and nobody would tell him anything. It was quite obvious they were covering up. So John said—it was about midnight— "I'm going to get in my car and go to Selma and find out about this." We all said, "John, you'll probably get killed, because there's nobody to protect you and there are probably a lot of gun-happy racists picking off people who've been to the Selma march." But John headed for Selma, fifty miles away, to get the story about Viola Liuzzo. He wasn't just a wonderful poet who wrote about real people and real things, but a dedicated human being as well. And he wasn't afraid to act.

SIXTEEN

Knowing Yourself

If you're going to take risks and be a democratic educator, you have to know about the situation you are working in. Some years ago I was asked to go to Kotzebue, Alaska, by the Northwest Arctic School District to help native Alaskan high school students and teachers make more use of the traditional people, the old folks, and try to learn some of their traditions. I told them I couldn't do that because I didn't know the situation. They asked me, "But how do you do it at Highlander?" And I said, "That won't do you any good, what we do at Highlander is based on knowing the culture of the people we are working with." But they kept insisting, and I said, "Well, first I'd have to know at least something about the people. If you want me to come up and do a week's seminar, I'll have to come up for two weeks so I know what I'm doing a seminar about. Then I can learn at least a little about the background of the people I'm doing a seminar for." They agreed and paid me to spend two weeks just going around and visiting. When the seminar took place I felt more comfortable, because I had lived in the native community for a few days.

On a recent trip to Australia and New Zealand, I was very careful all the time, in seminars and meetings to say, "I don't know anything about your situation and I'm not going to be here long enough to learn. I've read, and I've talked to people, but it's all foreign to my experience, different enough that I wouldn't know what to do. I'm not suggesting that you do any of the things that I'm talking about. I'm going to talk about what we do at Highlander, not what you should do. If there's anything in it that you want to ask questions about that I can discuss, that's fine."

The way I got to know about the situation of black people in the South and was therefore ready for the pre-civil rights period is a case in point. In the first place, I knew I wasn't black. So my relation to blacks was as a white who was concerned with problems of all people, and as a person who felt that the problems caused by whites were affecting whites as well as blacks. I believed that anything I want for myself, I must want for other people.

I didn't have any problem with saying to blacks, "All of us have problems that whites caused, but blacks will have to take the lead if the problems are to be dealt with. I will put Highlander at your disposal, and not try to share in making decisions. You've got to make the decisions, and if it doesn't violate our principles, we'll go along."

That way we had an honest basis of relating, and before long different groups of blacks came to Highlander to discuss their problems, because they thought the way we dealt with problems— asking questions and getting people to discuss them—would help. We were also in this position of trust because Highlander had always been open to black people.

In the first years, people like Dr. Charles Johnson, later the president of Fisk University, came to Highlander. Other people would visit and take part in the programs so the community and the students would get used to black people. The Highlander community also worked with black people in colleges and churches. I organized the first textile workers' union in the South under the CIO, and integrated it, even though I was instructed by Northern officials who had led racially mixed unions that we shouldn't integrate because they thought the South wasn't ready for it.

When we told black people we would put ourselves at their disposal, they took it seriously, because by that time we'd had black labor union students at Highlander. They knew we had demonstrated our belief and practice in social equality.

You have to be careful not to think that you're somebody else. I've had to avoid thinking that I'm Nicaraguan or, when I was in India, that I was Indian. I have a tendency to want to identify with people. I have to say to myself, "Look, Horton, get as close to people as you can, have as much interest as you can, but don't get things mixed up. You're white, and black people can't say they are color-blind. Whites and white-controlled institutions always remind them that they're black, so you've got to recognize color." This doesn't mean that you feel superior, it's just that you've got to recognize that you can never fully walk in other people's shoes. You can be only a summer soldier, and when the excitement is over, you can go back home. That doesn't mean that you don't have solidarity with black people and aren't accepted; it just means that you have a different role to play.

I think like a white person but try to understand how black people might think. If I'm not going to be a racist, I've got to understand as much as I can about other people's ways of thinking. Their way of doing things can be better than my way, can be worse than my way, but I can't take the position that my way is always right without being a racist. Racism involves believing that your own race is superior.

Most blacks I knew accepted me as a sincere person who was willing to accept them as equals. This acceptance gave me the freedom to be critical and to disagree. I used to do this whenever Martin Luther King, Jr., argued with me about nonviolence. He'd say, "Myles, you don't go all the way with nonviolence, you've got reservations." I'd say, "Yes, I've got reservations." For all practical purposes, I supported the nonviolence of the civil rights movement. It would have been counterproductive, in my opinion, to use violence; but philosophically, I reserved the right to say that at times

195

I might be for violence in a revolutionary situation. He used to kid me and say, "Well, we're going to get you to love everybody one of these days," and I'd say, "When they get worth loving, I'll love them."

I didn't mind speaking out. I used to raise questions about the lack of economic democracy, and the need to support organized workers and advocate for higher wages for low-paid workers. I said, "This capitalist society is not good enough for white people, and it sure as hell isn't good enough for blacks to struggle to get into."

I never hesitated to raise questions. And people didn't resent it, and they weren't afraid to oppose me. They not only opposed me at times, but they'd take a completely different line from the one I was advocating. I actually didn't have much influence, but this didn't keep me from trying to help.

Many people we worked with during the period of the civil rights movement had been at Highlander before it started. They knew what I believed and they knew what I'd done and they'd say, "Long before we thought we could do anything, Myles was trying to do something. He kept drawing us out and challenging us and trying to make us think." Alexander Meiklejohn once said, "No idea is any good unless it serves some useful purpose," and I used the best method I had of presenting ideas—not talking about them, but acting on them. People learn faster from action than from anything else. There was no hidden agenda, nothing people didn't know about, so we could agree or disagree without destroying our relationship.

You can't be accepted by people if you're trying to be what you're not. You've got to be genuinely what you are, but from what you are you've got to have empathy with and understanding of people and their situations, and you've got to relate as human beings in such a way that color isn't a factor in the relationship.

Once when I was in New Mexico working with Spanish-speaking people and Native Americans, a Native American complained to me about some of the people who were moving there in large numbers from California and other places. "You know," he said, "these people are going to tear up this country. They've got no sense. They pay a thousand dollars for a place that we used to be able to get for a hundred. We won't ever be able to buy land anymore. They don't understand what they're doing. The worst thing is, they dress like us and never take baths. I told some of them the other day, 'If you're going to imitate Native Americans, take a bath! We take baths!' " This is an extreme case, but even somebody who doesn't try to identify with poor people by dressing poor can still go back home or use a credit card. There's always an escape. That's perceived by poor people as being a lark. Whether they're doing it for the experience or from guilt, it's always slightly artificial.

When acting out of guilt, you're trying to get rid of the guilt, and that means you're trying to serve yourself, not the other people. That's never very constructive. I recognize that my own ancestors killed Native Americans and stole their land. One of them, as far as I can find out, may have been a slave trader who brought the first slave into Tennessee, so if I were in the guilt business, I should feel guilty. I know my ancestors were wrong, and I feel that what they did was evil and a great injustice—I wish they hadn't done it—but I personally don't feel guilty for their actions. I accept the guilt of the white race, but I don't feel Myles Horton is personally guilty.

SEVENTEEN

Learning from the Birds

People use "That's for the birds" in a derogatory sense, but I have learned valuable things from birds. I've learned that instinctively they know north and south; they know where to go in the wintertime, where to go in the summer. Birds will take advantage of a tail wind, and when the wind is blowing the other way, they'll hole up. They won't exhaust their strength going against that wind for long when they'd make only a few miles a day or get blown backward. They rest, because if they rest that day and restore their strength, the next day they can much more than make up for what they lost by not going.

As I read about birds, I realized that they not only use tail winds but they don't fight the winds. They change their course year after year on the basis of the particular situation. They never come back exactly the same way twice because the conditions are never the same, but they always get to their destination. They have a purpose, a goal. They know where they are going, but they zigzag and they change tactics according to the situation. I thought, for God's sake they're pretty smart, why can't we learn not to do things when it's almost impossible? Why can't we learn to hole up and renew our strength? Why can't we learn to change the entire route if it's necessary, so long as we get to the right point? I started learning from the birds about how to conserve energy and how not to wear myself out. I also learned how to take advantage of crisis situations and of the opposition and use that knowledge for my own purposes. Once I did that, it became a little easier to program ideas and survive, and to begin to share that kind of thinking with other people in a way they could understand.

Then it was easy to do the next thing I had learned: when you have an idea for something and you can't figure out an approach to the problem, you can talk it over with other people and get help on your ideas, even though they may not be of interest to them. I had known this for years, but I had to go through a period of getting some of these things straight in my mind before I could use them.

People, especially those who act out of guilt or who are recent converts, get principle mixed up with strategy. They learn it all as a package, and they think, "You believe this, and you do it this way." They feel that they would be betraying their principles if they didn't do something a particular way. People must be helped to understand that strategy is different from principle, that you've got to find a creative way to get what you're aiming at. If you're locked in a room and have to get out, you're not going to just stand there and rattle the door. You're going to try to find another way to escape from that room. Maybe you'll manage to force the lock, or you might break a window. You won't spend any time saying, "Well I've got to find the correct way to do it," because that's impossible. You'll have to find another way.

If you set out on a program and discover that your analysis is wrong, then you change, instead of spending all your energy trying to break that door down. You sit down and start thinking, and if you can't come up with a way to do it, you go fishing. Or read a poem, or look at the garden. You just quit for the time being, hole up and return to it later, when you're rested. That's what meditation does, it gets your mind off what you're doing so that you're freed up to come back at things with a fresh look.

Now sometimes even birds make the wrong analysis and fly into a storm. They have to fly against the wind, but after a while they stop fighting it and find a place to land and hole up. They don't try the impossible. I think that's very important in movements. There are times when you can't go ahead. It's not within your power to deal with it, because the forces out there are such that you can't. You're not superhuman, and it's beyond your power. That's the time to hole up and start thinking. You watch the wind, and wait for it to blow your way.

It took a lot of courage for me to learn to say, "I just don't understand this, I can't do it." Early on, I simply didn't have the courage to say, "I don't know how to deal with this problem, there's nothing I can do." I'd keep fuddling around and trying, hoping that I could hit on something, hoping that somebody would say something to get me out of it. I finally learned, however, that when I come to an impasse, there's nothing wrong with saying, "Look, I don't have the slightest idea how to deal with this problem. This is all I can think of, and it's just a waste of time for us to keep on talking about it, because I can't do anything about it. You can continue to talk about it, that's fine, but I can't. If you want to ask a question about it, about what I've discussed, about what I believe—anything—you ask me, I'll answer it. Or I'll tell you I can't answer it." I sometimes get questions to which I respond, "I'm sorry, I don't know anything about that, what I'd be doing is just guessing. Let's talk about something else." I learned that you don't have to pretend everything is something you can solve. Instead, you hole up like the birds until you get something you can deal with.

There were a lot of ideas that I never had the chance to test at Highlander. I'd like to have found a way for students to do more creative and intellectual work. I'd like to have seen the students reading more, but I was never able to work that out. People who came to Highlander had problems and were in a hurry to solve them. Reading has always been so important to me, that I've always believed that if I could get people used to reading more, I could help them to learn more. I don't mean shop reading (reading for a purpose), but reading poetry, literature, philosophy, science—anything. The trouble is that when you help people solve specific problems, there are so many other things you can't do.

Once, during the 1930s or early 1940s, I decided to have a two-week library session at Monteagle, in which people could come and take advantage of their leisure time just for the pleasure of reading. I would give guidance if they asked. I couldn't get anyone to come. I advertized the session, publicized it, said it would be very inexpensive. Nobody came. If I had said there would be a library session on how to do something specific, they would have attended, but just to have people come and read and learn never worked.

EIGHTEEN

Nicaragua

I've always wanted to see a country during the beginning stages of a revolution, and after an abortive effort to follow up my visit to Cuba three months after their revolution, I was determined to try to see something of the Nicaraguan revolution that overthrew Somoza in 1979. I was first invited to Nicaragua in 1980 to witness the return to Managua of the thousands of people who had been teaching reading in the countryside during the literacy campaign. It was very inspiring to see the young people coming back from the rural areas having learned more themselves than they had taught

International Conference on Popular Education for Peace, Nicaragua, 1983. *Highlander.*

the local people. That's not to minimize the terrific results of the campaign. I also came back very enthusiastic about the prospects of the development of a mixed economic society.

Five years before, I had been in Brazil and Peru to explore the possibility of gathering adult educators from all parts of the Americas, but I couldn't get an invitation to meet in any country south of the United States border. I was determined not to be a part of another North American–led gathering. After I returned from my first visit to Nicaragua, an invitation was made by the vice minister of the Ministry of Adult Education to hold the meeting in Nicaragua. After some time the invitation was firmed up, and the vice minister suggested that we first have a planning session at Highlander for the people sponsoring and planning the conference. In addition to the Ministry of Adult Education in Nicaragua, the sponsors were the Latin American Council of Adult Education (headed by Paulo Freire), the International Council for Adult Ed-

John Gaventa, Myles Horton, Dian Marino at the International Council for Adult Education Conference, Paris, 1982. *Highlander. Daniel Casseli.*

ucation and Highlander. Highlander staff members Sue Thrasher, Jane Sapp, John Gaventa and I went to Managua, and after a week at the conference, we visited other parts of the country, following up the contacts we'd made there. The people in Nicaragua called the meeting the International Conference on Popular Education for Peace. When we got down there, we found banners in the capital with a list of all the sponsors. It was a big thing for them, featured on television and in the newspapers.

One of the main purposes of the conference was to get people from the Americas acquainted with each other so that those of us on the adult education leadership level could recruit people from our various countries—people who worked in unions, cooperatives and social action groups of various kinds—to help facilitate the exchange of working people throughout these countries. As an example, before we left Nicaragua, one of the people who came from the United States, John Zippert of the Federation of Southern Cooperatives (an organization of black farmers in Mississippi), ar-

ranged for a counterpart from the Nicaraguan cooperative movement to speak at their next convention. That has been followed up
by fifteen to twenty exchange visits between people in the United
States, Central and South America. We laid the groundwork for a
continuing relationship, but the conference members agreed that
we wouldn't have another inter-American meeting—we didn't want
to start another organization, but to have regional meetings and get
together on specific issues. Half a dozen of these have taken place
since that time.

In Nicaragua there was a real follow-up to the initial literacy
crusade. Some of the people who learned to read and write in that
first crusade taught others as well. They had built a big organization
of noncertified teachers who were proud of the fact that they remained outside the academic educational system. In fact, a big
banner appeared during a demonstration of popular educators, saying, "We're not certified, we're educators." Now these people are
trying to bring popular education into the schooling system. That
means they'll deal with practical problems along with other formal
academic ones, and the students can use information as they learn
it, instead of saving it up for exams.

An example of how the Nicaraguans go about learning can be
seen in the way they planned their elections. When they decided
to have elections, they asked countries throughout the world to
send their election procedures so they could analyze them. Almost
every country complied except for the United States. The Nicaraguans ended up with a synthesis of the different forms of elections
around the world. Some countries also cooperated in other ways.
The Swiss government, for example, printed the ballots as a gift.

Two years after the International Conference on Popular Education for Peace, I was invited back as an official witness for the
elections. The Nicaraguan government invited newspaper people
and educators, and gave us full credentials to walk into the polling
places, look in the ballot boxes to see if they had been stuffed in
advance and to help count the ballots. I chose to go up near the
Honduran border and observe in the rural areas there. Part of our
time was spent in Ciudad Sandino, one of the places we had visited
before. The day I was there, seven people were killed by the Contras
within three miles of the city.

During the election, we could do everything but go behind the curtain when people were voting. Nobody could. Then that night we helped count the votes. A triple system is used to check the voters. Roughly 80 percent of the people registered, and over 80 percent of those registered actually did vote. The winning party had about a 60-percent plurality. Any group that could get together a certain number of members and hold a convention could be an official party, provided their position wasn't to overthrow the country by force. That was the only limitation. Some parties formed with a very small number of people just a month before the deadline. The old Communist party got the smallest number of votes, but they had equal time with all the other parties on radio, television and in the press, and it was all paid for by the government. It was illegal to spend more money than the government allotted.

Visiting Nicaragua has been my chance to follow up the demonstration against the invasion by the United States Marines that I attended in 1929 and to witness the beginnings of what could by now have been a successful follow-up to a revolution if it hadn't been for the United States support of the Contras and our other efforts to keep the country from developing.

In Nicaragua the government is trying to work out a mixed economy of socialist and free enterprise policies and principles, and to create a synthesis of the two. Right now the majority of Nicaraguan farms, land and industry are in individual, not state ownership. A lot of regulations guide their actions, so it's a blend of capitalism and socialism, and there's also a mixture of nationalism and religion. Many things come together in Nicaragua. The group that is really in power there is made up of several intellectuals— poets, writers, religious leaders—some of whom are students of Marxism. They try to combine all these elements in the government. For example, they're trying to learn how to pick the best of all the different economies. It's interesting to me, because this is as near as we can get to the place where socialism can be seen working itself out, and where we can begin to see what works and what doesn't.

NINETEEN

Who Really Owns the Land?

The current use of participatory research at Highlander is an example of the principle of doing things democratically in an international context. In earlier days there were similar activities at Highlander involving nonacademic research. We referred to them as action research because they constituted a form of collective action on problems defined by the people who were affected. Action research was used during the 1950s to involve people in the study of racial problems, in the farmers' union cooperatives and in other ways. Participatory research is defined by different people in different ways, but there are some universal characteristics. It is an investigation and an analysis of a problem by a group of people whose lives are directly affected by that problem. Ideally, their investigation will lead to action. Participatory research differs from the more conventional kind done by experts, usually identified with universities, in that it doesn't take decision making away from the people. Instead of becoming dependent on experts, the people become experts themselves.

Juliet Merrifield and her husband, John Gaventa, who is currently director of Highlander, have attempted to create a program of research that is consistent with Highlander's educational ideas. For them, research, like education, must grow from the problems of the people, not from problems in the researcher's head. It should be more than simply "technical assistance" or "backup."

Highlander has always tried to get people to do their own research, just as we tried to get them to learn from their own experience. This follows the belief that they can do things for themselves. It is empowerment. The people responsible for starting some of this research are professionals who have decided they want to use their talents to help others become researchers of their own problems.

One of the biggest problems in Appalachia is the lack of housing. This is the most densely inhabited rural area in America. People can't find anyplace to build houses because the land is all owned by large private and corporate interests that won't sell to individuals. People who came to Highlander were always wondering exactly who owned all this land. They kept asking questions about land ownership, and John Gaventa and some other people at Highlander finally said, "If you're interested in finding out, there is a way. We can start a research project, teach you how to do the research and together we can find out who owns the land." They started the Appalachian Land Ownership Task Force. Some of the people who volunteered were uneducated, some had secondary education, others were university professors. Anybody interested was welcome to help out. People were brought to Highlander for training in research methods, and then they organized themselves on a state basis with a state director. They got funds for the research, the funds were turned over to the state directors and these people got the information. They went to courthouses and searched through records. They learned, for example, that the sign outside the coal company has absolutely nothing to do with who owned it. Sometimes they had to trace through four or five steps before determining who the owner was. It might be an oil consortium—Exxon, for instance—or it might be a foreign owner. They learned who really owned the land, not just the names of the people on the records. It turned out that over 80 percent of the land was absentee-owned and that the tax rate on it was just a fraction of the tax rate on what little land the people owned. For example, the coal company that made $100 million profit didn't pay enough taxes to buy a school bus. The people didn't have buses and roads because there was no tax base, and the reason these large absentee landowners didn't pay taxes was that they controlled the judges, the governors—they controlled everything. That was all discovered in the process of this study.

Before the participatory research was finished, people were so incensed by what they were finding—and so empowered by knowing how to get information—that they started organizing. In Alabama, a number of absentee coal mine owners had gotten a bill introduced that would reduce their already low tax rate and it was about to be passed. As a result of the land study and subsequent organizing the bill was defeated. The people who had organized then started a process by which they got taxes increased. This was all done because the people there were involved in the study. Some other people set up an organization in Kentucky to deal with the tax problems. Later they began to focus on strip mining. The absentee owners were just destroying the environment so this group pushed to have a bill introduced in the legislature and started a court case. There are many examples of people starting to act as a result of being involved in the land study. One county paper in Kentucky published the entire study verbatim over a period of three months, and it was read all over Appalachia.

To my way of thinking, the most important thing was that these people got a sense of their own power to do something, and could then use that method to research any kind of problem.

Before the Land Study was finished and published, some people who were also involved in trying to get more programs in the schools went to their county board of education, where they were told there wasn't any money available. They came down to Highlander with some other people who had the same problem, and they figured out how they could legally demand to see the school records. Then they went in and did their own bookkeeping and found out there was plenty of money. They went back and said, "You told us that if you had the money . . . well, here it is, it's in the records, you've just been hiding it." A lot of things like that happened. These are people who never thought of themselves as researchers.

The Land Study and participatory research are constantly used in connection with programs to try to help people deal with their economic problems in the region: problems created by unemployment, plant and mine closures, and where jobs are available at all, problems caused by the trend to replace high-paying work with low-paying jobs.

In the early part of 1986 I was slightly involved in an international aspect of the participatory research exchange among countries, when the Society for Participatory Research in Asia invited me to be present in Delhi at the fourth birthday of their organization. They also arranged for me to visit members of their Asian organizations in other parts of India, and in Malaysia and the Philippines. While on that trip, I also went to visit people in New Zealand and Australia who had started programs that were similar in some ways to the work being done at Highlander.

In India they considered that participatory research should be composed of three interrelated processes: a collective investigation of problems with the participation of the constituents in the entire process; a collective analysis in which the constituency develops a better understanding not only of the problems but of their underlying structures and causes; and collective action by the same people aimed at solutions to the problems. In practice these three processes cannot be separated. Their integration gives participatory research its fundamental strength, although it takes different forms in different countries. You can see definite similarities in the way they're described.

The Gaventa family had just returned from a long stay in India when the tragic gas leak at the Union Carbide plant in Bhopal occurred. John and Juliet had gone to India to do some work with people involved in participatory research and John gave them a call and they decided to collaborate on publicizing and linking up what happened in India with conditions in the United States. The Gaventas had already made a videotape of the participatory researchers, and they updated it to include the Bhopal situation. In this country they went to Institute, West Virginia, where Union Carbide has a plant identical to the one in India and got the people there to talk so they could put the stories of both places together on tape. Then they made the tape available to people in India and the United States so they could see the same tape. This was followed by visits to Highlander by Indians involved in the Bhopal disaster.

That exchange set in motion a real learning experience and helped to bring together people from different countries who were working on similar problems. It is a perfect illustration of our need to deal with problems on an international basis, because of the international nature of capitalism.

On a recent trip to India I took part in a number of conferences and seminars in New Delhi, during which I shared a variety of the experiences of Appalachia and the South, and learned about some of the problems facing the Indian people. Then I went to Bombay to visit one of the groups in the Indian participatory research association—the Society for Promotion of Area Resources Centers—which had been organized a year or two before. It's made up largely of women in social work or popular education who are interested primarily in helping the invisible people who live on the sidewalks. Known as "pavement dwellers," they work for very low wages. They scavenge for paper, tin and plastic, building houses right on the sidewalks in sections of Bombay. These people have been looked on as outcasts and undesirables. The group of women who invited me there had carried on a participatory research project with those people, in which they took a census to find out how many there were, what kinds of jobs they had, how they survived, where they came from. I was there shortly after the survey had been concluded. These street people told me what they had learned about their own condition and about some of the plans for action that had grown out of the participatory research project. It's a good example of how people can become empowered, through their own involvement in problem solving, to plan collective action aimed at changing their lives for the better.

TWENTY

Many Highlanders

If there are places anywhere in the world where educational centers or research programs have been started by people who have been at Highlander and they want to have a relationship not only with Highlander but with other people who are doing similar things around the world, then I'd like to be of help in connecting them. That's a role which I have the time and freedom to do these days, now that I have retired from the Highlander staff.

Many people from all over the world have been to Highlander. They think it is doing a good job and they've wanted to see if they

Myles Horton, Paulo Freire, Highlander, 1987. *Highlander. Thorsten Horton.*

could adapt it to their own country. They've created centers which are all residential, deal with social issues and use unconventional educational methods. There are dissimilarities, but every one of them, including the most recent one (started in Chile), focuses on out-of-school education for working people or aboriginal people. They're informal. The people who run them say they've gotten a lot of ideas from Highlander. All of them are involved in the International Adult Education Association, and all except the Australian people are involved in participatory research.

When we established Highlander, Don West and I were sure there would be Highlanders in every state. A dozen or more attempts to start Highlanders were made in this country, but none succeeded. My analysis for some time has been that Highlander is a Third World idea. It has worked in Appalachia and the South because they have a lot in common with Third World countries or Third World segments within other countries.

Myles Horton, Zilla Hawes, one of the earliest staff members, at Highlander's fiftieth anniversary, 1982. *Highlander. Deborah Barndt.*

Over the past few years I've visited a number of these centers and have helped connect them with each other. After my trip to India to visit with some of the participatory researchers that Juliette Merrifield and John Gaventa work with, I went to Malaysia, where I visited some of the workers on the unionized rubber plantations. In Malaysia the top people are the Malaysians, the next group is made up of Chinese and the people at the bottom originally came from India. The Indians make up most of the work force on the plantations. The group I visited was very independent, and they managed to defy the union whenever it didn't seem to serve them. They said the president of the union was tied in with the government negotiations. He negotiated with the owners and signed contracts for wage increases or decreases—whatever the situation was—and the workers could never find out what the conditions were because he never allowed them to see the contracts. The group I visited was interested in how Highlander worked to help create democratic unions.

On my trips I go to colleges, speak at conferences and meet with workers. Everyone works the socks off me. That's the way I learn best. I couldn't do this when I was director of Highlander because I couldn't get away—somebody would raid the school or something and I'd have to fly back in a hurry. Now I can go anywhere and stay as long as I want. My trips are not part of a Highlander program in the sense that they're Highlander-financed. They're my volunteer efforts to help an international part of the current Highlander program that I'm very much interested in and want to see expanded.

The transnationals have created one world for business, and we have sought to create one world for people. I have been trying to help create this kind of world so we can deal with world capitalism. If you had world socialism, you'd still have problems of trying to work out relationships and iron out problems. It's just that now the world is dominated by the capitalists, and that's why we have to concentrate on this problem.

Several years ago, Aline Balaminde, an official of a Philippine organization that works with small farmers, came to Highlander. I think she was sent here by the agricultural mission section of the U.S. Council of Churches. She later became interested in participatory research and met in Yugoslavia with John Gaventa and other people from the U.S. When my India trip was planned by the participatory research group in Asia, she was the contact person in the Philippines who arranged my visit there.

I had a reservation on the first U.S. plane that left for the Philippines after Corazon Aquino's inauguration, so I was fortunate to arrive in Manila while the excitement was still very high and the city very hopeful. I soon took off for Negros, where the story was completely different. There was great enthusiasm for Aquino and the few people who were still working in the sugarcane plantations said, "Well, it may be all right for the city people, but not for us. We just read it in the paper." The political prisoners I talked to in Negros said, "No, they're not going to let us out, they're going to turn a few name people out." They were right; they are still in prison.

In Negros I stayed at the headquarters of the National Federation of Sugar Workers, a very simple sort of office building, but they had one little room about the size of a large table that had two bunk beds in it. The bunks were planks; there was no padding, no give in the planks. It was kind of hard on my bones, but I found that by taking newspapers and folding them eight to ten times, I could get the planks to feel like a mattress. I was right there where I could go out to the communities with the organizers, talk to the workers and get a better understanding of the situation. I stayed at the headquarters two or three days, and then I got them to take me out for two nights to live where the union members were and to visit some of the local offices.

Since the bottom dropped out of the sugar market and those huge estates no longer even grow any sugar, the owners have kicked the people off the land and employed guards, supplemented by the army, to keep them from coming back and using the land to grow things to live on. The people I stayed with were living in a kind of swamp on the side of the road, surviving on roots and frogs and things like that. They didn't have anything else to eat. I asked the organizer who went with me to advise what we should take, and he said, "Beans and rice. They don't have anything. If you want anything to eat, you take it with you." I also took some fruit, which I knew would be a great delicacy. It was the first fruit they said they'd had in a year.

Everyone slept on mats on the floor, but the floors there are built out of reeds, so they give. There are wild animals and pigs underneath the elevated floor, but that floor was like a featherbed compared to what I'd been sleeping on. I enjoyed being there and talking to these people, talking with the kids and getting acquainted with them. It was hard to accept that these people couldn't get on the estates and grow things on the land. They wouldn't have hurt the land, they just weren't allowed on it. That situation hasn't changed since I was there.

The area where the sugar workers lived is the center of the Communist-led New People's Army. It was soon apparent that most of the people I talked to were sympathetic to that army, so of course I had to be careful about asking questions. Probably a lot of them were Communist guerrillas. It's the place where the New People's Army has grown most rapidly in recent years. The reason for that rapid growth is easy to understand when you realize that this area used to be the center of employment in the sugar industry, and now for the last few years there have been no jobs. What the Communists demand is that the people be allowed full access to the land they once lived on, since it isn't being used for anything else—hardly a revolutionary demand. But there's a resistance, because the landowners are afraid that if they allow the people to use the land, they will take over. Now Mrs. Aquino promised land reform (she belongs to one of the five biggest landowning families), and she said that her family and others would share their land, but the proposal that she's made to the legislature is for the government to buy the land from the landowners and sell it on a long-term basis to the people that used to work there. That would require the government to float bonds and borrow millions and millions of dollars, and it would require the approval of the World Bank and the United States government, so the mild land reform that she's proposing is not going to solve the problem any time within the next few years.

In Mindanao, one of the larger islands, there is a strong anti-army and antigovernment movement in which some of the local priests are participants. I visited a social work organization that hosted my stay there, and they took me out to a place which used to be a fishing village. The people have more or less taken it over. They moved out there and started restructuring their lives. They had a little factory where they made soap, another place where they were making candy to sell. It's a pretty place, so they also had a small tourist industry. This little village was a very hopeful place that people came from all over the world to visit. You could buy candy, soap, visit with the people. They even had a co-op.

When I was there, I met a woman from Holland who knew all about Highlander. We started talking to people about the civil rights movement, and they got terribly excited. Since they were all interested, we asked if they'd ever had any discussions about things like that, and they said, "Oh yes, we meet every week and have these kinds of discussions." They knew about the civil rights movement and wanted to learn more. It was so exciting to see these people begin to take over this little village and build up their lives. Since then, unfortunately, the government army has moved into that town. They took the little soap factory, closed it down and used it for a barracks. They also shut the candy factory and some of the people left and others now work for the army. They just moved in and destroyed that village. As far as I know, there's nothing much left in this area of Mindanao or Negroes that's going to help much with the overall problem.

When I got back to Manila, it was a different story. You could see euphoria. One of the founders of the Communist party had just been released along with some of the other top people in the country, and there were promises that everybody would be let out of prison. I even heard a man who had organized the Communist party and had been let out of jail talk about having hope for cooperation between the Communist party and the government. My experiences had been very different in the outlying islands, where most of the people live, but it was very educational to be that close to a radical or revolutionary change. It was a fundamental change brought about by a coalition of the church, a lot of the middle-class people who hated Marcos because he'd done them in, working people and one faction of the army. However, if nothing happens in the way of land reform, the future looks dim.

From the Philippines I went to Australia to visit Margaret Valadian, who had come to Highlander in 1973. She is an aborigine and the first woman from her tribe to graduate from college. While she was at Highlander, we spent a lot of time talking about her people and about what was going on at our school. When Margaret went back, she started working on what she called their version of Highlander. The program that she set up is located in New South Wales in an old building which the Catholic church used to run as a home and a center. They have meetings somewhat like we have at Highlander, and they bring people in from the aboriginal back country and have a variety of educational programs that deal with the problems of her people. She told me, "We have come close to losing the aboriginal community as a viable, healthy, contributing sector in this country. We're now well down the path toward what is going to be a total dependent welfare community. If you destroy people's rights to accountability, to performance, to responsibility, then all you can create in return is a total welfare-dependent community. You prostitute the dependency." Along with her co-worker, Natasha McNamare, she tries to deal with these enormous problems. Unfortunately, I didn't have time to go to the back country where many of the aboriginal people live, where Margaret and Natasha had come from, but I spent a whole day looking at videos of their workshops and their life in the country, and I had the chance to get a feel for what was going on.

While I was there, they arranged for a seminar called "Education for All, the Non-Formal Way," and I led discussions on a wide range of problems, including those I had witnessed in other parts of Asia and during my visit to South Africa the year before. In addition to working with their own people, they drew individuals from the government and various organizations. Margaret has been trying for several years to link Highlander-type groups around the world, another example of how some of the ideas that developed at Highlander have taken different forms and spread, becoming the basis of programs in other countries that use some of the original ideas and add others of their own.

One of the things I talked about was South Africa. The year before, I had visited Wilgespruit, a residential center on the edge of Soweto which is quite similar to Highlander. It's run by Dale and Tish White. Dale is an Episcopalian minister and his church is a thousand-member black church in Soweto. He's quite a national figure in opposition to the present government. Through Wilgespruit I was able to meet people in Soweto and in a number of other parts of South Africa—down in the southern part, up on the border near Mozambique and Botswana—and get some sense of what was going on there.

I was taken to a South African Council of Churches meeting which had recently been chaired by Bishop Tutu, whom I met later at another meeting. The people welcomed me the morning I arrived by singing "We Shall Overcome," and in the afternoon I sang it again with a group of black and white people.

The most exciting part of my visit to South Africa was getting acquainted with the black miners' movement, to me the most encouraging development that I encountered in 1985. Black miners have set up their own union because they were never accepted on a full basis with the white workers' union. White mine employees in the diamond and coal industry get five times the salary of blacks, so the black miners organized their own union and were just beginning to make demands. I met some people there at the center who were hiding out after leading a wildcat strike. One of them had his collarbone broken, and another had a broken leg. Some had been beaten up. From these men and from others, I got a feeling that the black miners' union showed as much promise as anything else in the struggle. Since that time, the world has learned about their strike. I came to another conclusion that the apartheid government would continue to make gestures only, little cosmetic changes, to try to deflect the opposition from the outside world, but that they wouldn't make any changes to alter the structure of the government. They would attempt to combine what seemed to be forms of appeasement with brutality, to try to keep the blacks in check.

While I was in South Africa there were a lot of student uprisings, not so much in Soweto but in Alexander and other places nearby. The authorities were brutalizing the students in an attempt to force them back into school, and the students were getting more and more radicalized by the process.

I met with some wonderful black-sash groups, organizations of white women who oppose apartheid, that were trying to help people who had problems arising from the oppressive situation. Other women's groups, both black and white, were also involved, but I had a feeling that they would never be able to get any basic changes. These would have to come from the black people's radical action in forcing the issue.

I also got a feeling that we in North America have a lot to learn from the people there, as we do from all Third World situations. In South Africa the whites are a "First World" group, the blacks members of a Third World group, right in the same country. The lessons from the struggles that are going on there could be very helpful to us if we would identify ourselves with the people and learn something about the resistance they're putting up and their fight for the simple right to vote, which I predicted then, and still feel, will be denied them. I don't believe that the white government will voluntarily give black people the right to vote on an equal basis with white voters. It will continue a policy of setting people up in their own so-called "homelands," allowing them to vote there but not in South Africa.

Since that visit, just as after my visit to India, there has been an exchange. The people who run Wilgespruit, Dale and Tish White, and some of their coworkers have been to Highlander, as well as some people I met in Soweto, and Highlander staff members Helen Lewis and Lucy Phenix have visited South Africa. One of the activists here in the mountains, Rich Kirby, who lives up in Dungannon, Virginia, has made two trips to South Africa and is working very hard to do something about the situation there by raising funds and organizing anti-apartheid activities. So this contact with

South Africa has been another link in the chain of people in the United States and other countries learning from each other.

I went to South Africa to learn what I could. I didn't want to get into trouble there, or to cause any trouble. I wanted to keep a low profile and never spoke or made any public statements, although some people in the press found out I was visiting, and they learned something about who I was. I refused to do anything publicly because I wanted to keep moving, rather than be expelled from the country. Theoretically, it's illegal for a white person to go into Soweto without a pass. Blacks can't leave without one. Although the law is not enforced on whites regularly, it's there to be used by the authorities if they so choose, and since I wasn't about to ask for a pass, I could have been picked up any time quite legally. I tried to avoid that by keeping a low profile. I knew I was being watched sometimes, but I decided I wasn't going to do anything to make it easier. On my last day there I was going to leave early, but Dale White asked me if I'd speak in his church in Soweto. I figured that the word wouldn't spread from there until I had left the country, so I agreed. Everything was translated from English into two languages. There was the same kind of enthusiasm and wonderful singing that takes place in black churches in the South. I cautiously said that I had been involved in the civil rights movement and that the fight for freedom which had occurred in the United States was needed in other places. I spoke of my hope that one day they would make some of the limited gains which we had achieved in the United States through the civil rights movement. It was very low-keyed. I didn't do much more, but they all knew what I was talking about, and they started dancing and shouting. I just didn't want to get Dale or myself in trouble, so that was the only time I gave a public talk while I was there.

On my way to South Africa I had stopped off in London to visit friends, Judy and Herb Kohl. Herb and I decided to go to Belfast to talk with Tom Lovett and his family, who had previously been to Highlander for two months or so. When Tom left Highlander, he intended to go back and adapt some of the ideas he learned there to the situation in Belfast. At the time we went to Belfast, he had already started the Ulster People's College. It's a residential adult education center that focuses on trying to develop understanding between Protestants and Catholics, particularly in connection with

221

labor unions. We found it very inspiring and encouraging to see this new kind of institution developed by native residents of Belfast.

The last stop on my Asian trip was Auckland, New Zealand, where I went to visit John Benseman, who at that time was with the Workers' Education Association, a group based on the Workers' Education Bureau in England. He wanted to go beyond that, to work on a residential basis like Highlander and that was the reason he wanted me to come over. I was glad to accept the invitation because I not only wanted to find out what he was doing and see if I could be of any help to him, but I wanted to visit New Zealand because I was very much impressed with the country's stand against nuclear weapons and I wanted to know about the Maori. John arranged for me to do some seminars there connected with his program. The people who asked the best and most lively questions were the Maori, who were educated there.

These native people of New Zealand were reduced to poverty when the European settlers took their land away. I was told by the Maori that partly as a result of our civil rights movement they decided to have their own movement. By the time they decided to do that their land had all been taken away, and 80 percent of them lived in the cities. The remainder still lived in the country but not on their own land. The Maori knew that to have influence they had to achieve some status in the white world, so they started going to school, and now there are a lot of educated people among them. Many of them have entered the social structure and gotten government jobs.

At some formal meetings, I met some Maori who ran various programs. They were the ones who always asked the good questions.

Before long they started inviting me to come to their programs. They'd say, "This formal meeting is kind of dull, isn't it? You should come to my meeting. It'd be more like what you're talking about. You'll feel more at home there. People will appreciate you more."

One of the programs I visited was in a low-income community of mostly Maori people. The kids they worked with were dropouts and members of street gangs. They were running a literacy program for these teenagers and young adults. The young people were obviously bored with what I was talking about, and they weren't about to listen to this white character from the United States. I kept trying to figure out what to do. I couldn't get them to talk or do anything, which is just what happens with the college and high school kids in this country who sit there and wait for you to tell them something, and who have the same problem with their peers laughing at them. I just couldn't get to them. I was speaking about the civil rights movement and the struggles in the United States. I tried to talk about India and Africa. No response. Then I said, "My country is kind of like yours in some ways. You have a country with beautiful scenery. We have a country with beautiful scenery, but I can take a plane and in half a day see all the beauty spots in New Zealand. We have as much beauty, but it's scattered out more. You have a beautiful country . . . but the thing I like most about it is the courageous position you've taken as a nuclear-free country standing up against the United States." They all rose and cheered and hollered. The only time I got their attention was when I congratulated them for standing up against the big bullies. From then on I could have talked to them about potatoes and they would have listened. I was so surprised that would push the button needed to get to them.

Probably the most exciting thing that happened to me while I was there was that through John Benseman I was put in touch with a group of white educators who were working in a Maori educational program. They asked me to attend a seminar at Waikeo University in Hamilton, which specializes in the Maori. Through this group I got an invitation to visit a traditional gathering—the Maori have their own meetinghouses, their own traditional gathering places that go back to the very beginnings long before New Zealand was colonized. As far as I could find out, these gatherings are at the heart of the traditional Maori happenings today.

A warring group comes to the gathering in peace, presumably, but since no one can be certain, there is a ceremony of greeting and testing in the fenced-off compound where the people live. The elders speak friendly greetings and then sing, the men doing the talking and the women the singing. Next they talk and sing at each other and slowly move closer together. That way, they can determine whether the people in the other group have come as enemies or as friends. Finally, they get close enough that the visitors break from the ranks and offer a gift. Then the apologetic, halfhearted testing stops and the visitors are given a big welcome.

After the talking is over, all the people in the inviting group line up, and all the visitors go by and greet the hosts with nose kisses.

Once you've gone through that process, you're in; if others come later on, you're a host and they have to nose you to get in. Once the formalities are over there's feasting and much talk about traditions and current problems. A lot of these people are educated, some of them are government officials, some of them are just ordinary folk—it's just a delightful mix.

The meetinghouse consists of one big empty room. At night they have sleeping bag–sized mattresses which are spread on the floor. I found a place to sleep between a woman and a five-year-old child. They're so natural about it, but they've already checked you out. Once you've been invited, they never question you. I didn't know the ropes, however. That night I tried to figure out how I was going to remain on this little spot when I turned over—I sometimes like to sleep with my knees drawn up, stretch out and flop around. As I moved about, trying to get settled in, this beautiful middle-aged woman next to me said, "I won't attack you, you don't have to be so careful."

Before everyone goes to sleep they have a meeting and everybody sits up on their beds, the speakers at one end, and they talk about their traditions and things like that. Nobody can get up during a speech. There's a regular format. The men speak and the women sing, then people spin something around on strings to the rhythm of the music, so that all over the house these things are spinning to the music, and people are singing and having a very good time.

In this particular group the women were trying to organize and protest against the way women were treated—this was being done in the universities and everywhere else—so they brought this protest into the meeting, and it was interesting to see how they sabotaged the agenda. They weren't playing along or being very respectful of the traditions, and one of the old men got all upset. He simply wasn't going to have that, even though they were only agitating a bit. You could see they were getting ready to change things.

The next day was just like a Highlander workshop. There were seminar discussions about problems—about how their traditions were being denied them, how they were being mistreated and how they had to get sovereignty. There is a lot of literature coming out now about Maori sovereignty, and they told me a lot of that came as an outgrowth of the civil rights movement in the United States. Participating in these discussions was by far the most exciting thing I did while I was there.

• • • •

A year ago, while I was teaching for the University of Alaska at Kotzebue and at some other places around the state, I met a Maori woman on the same circuit. Our paths crossed twice and we had wonderful times together because she was so pleased to find somebody who knew about the Maori and New Zealand. It was very easy to relate their experience and problems to the native Alaskans. This is beginning to be part of my usable knowledge.

The transnationalists who make up the world's capitalist system are already First Worlders. I think the most important thing for me to do now is to make some kind of contribution to the bringing together of people in the Third World, both domestic and foreign, so that we can have some way of dealing with the world's capitalist system. We have to work with people on the same level on which they operate. People should be getting together on a world basis anyway, not just to counteract or deal with big business, but because that's what the world should be like. Highlander has always dealt with the poor, people who earn a living by what they do rather than by having ownership or control of wealth. That is the segment of society we have chosen to work with, so we just extend this concept to the world situation.

In order for Highlander to bring people from all over the world together with people from Appalachia and the South, they have to have common concerns and problems. Miners from places as different as Wales and Southern Africa have mining problems in common with Appalachian miners; health workers from Nicaragua or India have problems in common with health workers throughout the South. A more specific example of this worldwide concern for workers' problems is the common problems experienced by workers at Union Carbide's chemical plants in both Bhopal, India, and Institute, West Virginia.

When people have common interests they're more likely to learn more from their relationship. One role for places like Highlander now is to match up people with mutual backgrounds, concerns and goals. Their meetings should not only be a chance for them to visit each other but also to have real discussions and do analysis, so they can maximize their learning and take home things to do to solve their problems.

Now if I can help facilitate these meetings, I think my travels are worthwhile.

225

TWENTY-ONE

The Future

When I speak about a social goal, the goal for society, and for myself, I don't say, "This is exactly what it's going to be like." I don't have a blueprint in mind. I'm thinking more of a vision, I'm thinking of direction and I'm thinking of steps. I'm thinking more in terms of signs pointing in the right direction than I am of the shape of future society, because I don't know what that shape is going to be—I don't know of anybody who has predicted correctly. Marx, for example, who has probably been the most help to me in analyzing problems, wasn't a prophet or a seer. When he speculated

226

about what society would be, and how it would happen, he was frequently wrong. He was certainly wrong about where the revolution would first occur: It has taken place in countries where he said it wouldn't, and it's not taken place in countries where he said it would. The world has changed since he made his original analysis.

I think it's important to understand that the quality of the process you use to get to a place determines the ends, so when you want to build a democratic society, you have to act democratically in every way. If you want love and brotherhood, you've got to incorporate them as you go along, because you can't just expect them to occur in the future without experiencing them before you get there. I agree with Che Guevara: the true revolutionary is guided by great feelings of love. If that love isn't built in, you'll end up with a fascist society.

A long-range goal to me is a direction that grows out of loving people, and caring for people, and believing in people's capacity to govern themselves. The way to know they have these capabilities is to see something work well on a small scale. I've seen it in the labor movement, I've seen it in the civil rights movement, I've seen it in the antiwar movement. Since I know those things can happen on a small scale, I assume that if we ever get wise enough and involve enough people, it could happen on a bigger scale. If you have that hope, when you work with people and try to help them learn—and not teach them, because that gets into techniques and gimmicks—and you believe in them, then you inspire them by your belief. You can't help people grow if you don't think they can, because you are going to find ways to help prevent them from growing. I think your belief in people's capabilities is tied in with your belief in a goal that involves people being free and being able to govern themselves.

It is important to distinguish between this goal of freedom and self-governance and the goals of people who want only to "Save the whales" or to "Desegregate the South" or to organize a labor union. Those aren't necessarily long-range social goals. I don't mean they're antisocial, but the goal I'm talking about is one that can never be reached. It's a direction, a concept of society that grows as you go along. You could go out of business if you were only for saving the whales: you'd save them, then you'd be out of work. That would be the end of it. It's not that I'm against saving the whales. I'm all for it, but the reason for saving whales is that they

227

are a part of life, and you want to save life. You must make your goal a part of something larger. If it's an end-all, then it has severe limitations. A long-range goal has to be something for everybody. It can't be a goal that helps some people but hurts others.

Goals are unattainable in the sense that they always grow. My goal for the tree I planted in front of my house is for it to get big enough to shade the house, but that tree is not going to stop growing once it shades my house. It's going to keep on growing bigger regardless of whether I want it to or not. The nature of my visions are to keep on growing beyond my conception. That is why I say it's never completed. I think there always needs to be struggle. In any situation there will always be something that's worse, and there will always be something that's better, so you continually strive to make it better. That will always be so, and that's good, because there ought to be growth. You die when you stop growing.

Your vision will grow, but you will never be able to achieve your goals as you envision them. My vision cannot be achieved by me. You may save the whales, but the dream must push beyond that. It's a dream which I can't even dream. Other people will pick it up and go beyond. To put it in a simpler way, I once said that I was going to start out on a life's work. It had to be big enough to last all my life. And since I didn't want to have to rethink and start over again, I needed to have a goal that would at least take my lifetime. After making that decision, I never thought of doing anything else, because I knew that I could just hack away on it, and what little I could do would take my lifetime. And even if we had a revolution, the quality of that revolution wouldn't necessarily be satisfactory, so I'd have to try to make it better.

Name Index

229

About the Author

Myles Horton founded the Highlander Folk School in the 1930s and was its director for many years. Highlander is still flourishing today. Myles Horton died in 1990.

Herbert Kohl and Judith Kohl spent ten years working and traveling with Myles Horton. Herbert is the author of the bestselling *36 Children* and many other books in the field of education. Judith was the recipient of a National Book Award (1977) for *A View from the Oak*. They live in California.